A meticulously researched biography of the 19th-century Hindu mystic, Sri Ramakrishna Paramahansa, *Thakur* is a disciple's tribute to a guru – something that gives the book an intimate touch. The book traces Thakur's spiritual journey from childhood up to his death, focussing on significant moments, events and people that shaped his life. The writer helps us understand what made Thakur such a driving force in Indian philosophy. Numerous incidents and anecdotes enrich the book and make it a great read.

– *Hindustan Times,* New Delhi, 8 August 2008

This biography traces the life of one of India's greatest saints and the various powers he possessed with a lifelong communion with Goddess Kali .... It must have taken Mehrotra years of immense research to write this magnificent biography, but he has done full justice to this subject. To say that it is an illuminating work is to make an understatement .... This book tells how it all came about. And understandably [it] holds one spell-bound with the mystic unfolding of events.

– *Free Press Journal*, Mumbai, 12 July 2008

Mehrotra writes about his spiritual odyssey with all its emotional frenzy and strange transports in great detail, offering an in-depth look at the enormous complexity of the phenomenon of self-realization .... The narration is full of incidents and anecdotes and enlivened by Ramakrishna's penchant for humour .... A fine, intelligently written book that explores a complex subject with subtlety and skill.

– *Life Positive*, November 2008

Easily the most reader-friendly and yet comprehensive biography of this Great Master, endearingly titled as *Thakur – Sri Ramakrishna* .... Mehrotra's narrative gift is remarkably precise and richly evocative. It integrates all the details concerning an aspect into a visual and verbal complex of significance that is truly suggestive .... Mehrotra's inwardness with spirituality in its myriad forms, evident in his earlier book, *The Mind of the Guru*, and in his close association with H.H. The Dalai Lama and Swami Ranganathananda (who initiated him) attains in this book a remarkable manifestation. His racy style and turn of phrase and image, honed to exquisite evocative nuances of suggestion, make the book indispensable reading ...

– The Vedanta Kesari, September 2008

THAKUR
Sri Ramakrishna

A Biography

(Revised and Enlarged Edition)

Rajiv Mehrotra

HAY HOUSE INDIA
Australia • Canada • Hong Kong • India
South Africa • United Kingdom • United States

Hay House Publishers (India) Pvt. Ltd.
Muskaan Complex, Plot No.3, B-2 Vasant Kunj, New Delhi-110 070, India
Hay House Inc., PO Box 5100, Carlsbad, CA 92018-5100, USA
Hay House UK, Ltd., 292-B Kensal Rd., London W10 5BE, UK
Hay House Australia Pty Ltd., 18/36 Ralph St., Alexandria NSW 2015, Australia
Hay House SA (Pty) Ltd., PO Box 990, Witkoppen 2068, South Africa
Hay House Publishing, Ltd., 17/F, One Hysan Ave., Causeway Bay, Hong Kong
Raincoast, 9050 Shaughnessy St., Vancouver, BC V6P 6E5, Canada

Email: contact@hayhouse.co.in

The moral right of the author has been asserted.

(This book was earlier published under the title
Thakur: A Life of Sri Ramakrishna in 2008)

ISBN 978-81-89988-63-0

Designed and typeset at
Hay House India

Printed and bound at
Thomson Press (India) Ltd.

This book is dedicated to
the many masters and sentient beings
who through their patience, kindness and generosity
have helped me on my journey

in particular to

The late Swami Ranganathananda
His Holiness The Dalai Lama

and to the memory of

Har Narain & Shanti Mehrotra
Sarada Gopinath

and to

Meenakshi Gopinath

Contents

Foreword

*S*ri Ramakrishna was one of the great spiritual masters and mystics of all time. His life and strivings were transparent. Deeply rooted in the traditions and philosophies of India and its civilization, his message is for all time and for all people everywhere.

He has inspired not only great spiritual activists such as Swami Vivekananda who founded the Ramakrishna Mission to honour his master but also generations of monks, *sadhakas*, scholars and lay people around the world. In Sri Ramakrishna's universal teachings they have individually and collectively found pointers and lessons for their own spiritual growth and the inspiration to serve others. They have each emphasized and learnt from different facets of Sri Ramakrishna's religion.

Sri Ramakrishna was both divine and intensely human. It is difficult for any one human mind to fully understand and interpret the life of an avatar. Each account must therefore seem finally incomplete on its own. There have been several excellent biographies in Bengali, English and other languages, each from the vantage point of the author.

This effort through the prism of a serious lay spiritual aspirant grounded in tradition as he embraces the modern is a truly laudable contribution and addition to the literature on

Sri Ramakrishna. It offers important new perspectives and insights based on the imperatives of the twenty-first century and the author's personal quest.

Rajiv Mehrotra has long been a friend of the Ramakrishna Mission. He took Diksha from Swami Ranganathanandaji Maharaj, the thirteenth President of Ramakrishna Math and Ramakrishna Mission. With his blessings and support, and that of Swami Gokulananda and our Mission in Delhi he produced and presented a television series on the life of Sri Ramakrishna which was released by the then President of India Shri K.R. Narayanan at Rashtrapati Bhavan in the presence of Swami Ranganathanandaji Maharaj, Swami Gokulananda and other luminaries to great critical acclaim.

I wish his latest offering to Sri Sri Thakur all success, and invoke His blessings on him and all who read the book.

Swami Gahanananda
President
Ramakrishna Math and
Ramakrishna Mission
January 2007

Author's Note:

Swami Gahanananda Maharaj passed away in November 2007. He has been succeeded by Swami Atmasthananda.

Preface

This book is offered to the reader with great trepidation as 'my' book. Each time I go back to reading the text it feels like I was reading someone else's work. I didn't write this book. It got written. I believe I have been merely a blessed, undeserving intermediary. It draws upon the contributions, insights, writings and support of more people than I can conceivably acknowledge or recall. It is based on what began as a personal journey more than thirty-five years ago when as a teenager I attended the lectures of Swami Ranganathananda with my father in Calcutta. Swamiji was then a young monk and through his long and distinguished career that climaxed as President of the Ramakrishna Mission I was blessed by his wisdom and guiding hand in my quest. In the later years of his life he encouraged me to use my skills as a television anchor and filmmaker to produce a television series on the life of Sri Ramakrishna. While I struggled to research, understand and then write a script he gave me long hours of his valuable time drawing upon his wisdom and rich experience with the teachings of Sri Ramakrishna, occasionally leading me through practices that I might more fully experience and thus better communicate elements of the narrative. I was not a worthy student.

The television series was only a moderate success and went largely unnoticed in the cacophony of commercial television.

The manuscript for this book evolved as part of my continuing process of bringing order to my thoughts and understanding the profound relevance and lessons from the life of Sri Ramakrishna, a need to go beyond the brevity and simplification that writing for the visual media seemed to involve. I went back to a lifelong collection of notes. I had started collecting these much before I thought of a book or a television serial, for my own learning, memorizing and understanding. They were written while reading books, and listening to the monks of the order, especially Swami Ranganathananda. This work is also deeply indebted to the contributions of my friend Indira Rana who passed away while we were still researching the television series together. This book is really by all of them and the many authors and commentators I have read and learnt from over the years. I crave forgiveness from them all for not acknowledging individual contributions and sources. I have no records. I will be grateful to anyone who can help point out specific references or quotes so that these can be duly acknowledged in the future editions.

At the urgings of several monks of the Ramakrishna Mission but most of all my first editor Krishan Chopra, I found the courage to publish a work on a subject I know little about and that draws more on the works and insights of others than my own.

I am deeply grateful to the current President of the Ramakrishna Mission, Swami Atmasthananda; its late President Swami Gahanananda, Swami Prabhananda, the late Swami Gokulananda, Swami Atmashraddhananda, Swami Shantatmananda, Swami Bodhasarananda, and the many monks of the Ramakrishna Order who have inspired and helped me over decades and vetted the manuscript at different stages pointing out errors and making many valuable suggestions. The remaining errors, needless to add, are my own.

While evolving and fine-tuning the manuscript, I was helped enormously by the contributions of my sister Preeti Kapur, Milly

Chakravarthy, Bindu Badshah, Asha Sharma, Jehanara Wasi, Sherna Wadia and by Shalini Srinivas for her help with the supplementary research and in putting the glossary together.

I am profoundly greatful for the support and unequivocal encouragement of my current publisher Ashok Chopra and Hay House. This a second revised and somewhat expanded edition that includes an index, some minor corrections suggested by the Ramakrishna Mission, and photographs generously provided by them. It follows a modest first edition that quietly slipped into the market and sold out in a matter of a few weeks.

* * *

In my early thirties my quest led me to the footsteps of the Buddha and the teachings of His Holiness The Dalai Lama. Even though this evolved from a tradition of devotion to a 'creator' God to the agnostic world view of Buddhism, I continued to draw inspiration from the sadhanas of both the young Gadadhar who was to evolve to Sri Ramakrishna, as the young prince Siddhartha was to become the Buddha. That the latter became the primary inspiration for my journey did not diminish my celebration of the former. As my root guru The Dalai Lama teaches, we each have different mental dispositions, and hence have much to learn from different paths drawing upon different traditions to fulfil individual needs. These can change and evolve. No one path is inherently superior or inferior per se. We can and must learn from all of them, even as we remain true to the primary teaching that works best for us.

Sri Ramakrishna was to embody a similar aspiration and inspired people from diverse backgrounds who came to him – Tantrics, Vendantists, Christians, Muslims, Sikhs, Buddhists, *et al*. He said: 'With sincerity and earnestness one can realize God through all religions. The Vaishnavas will realize God, so will the Saktas, the Vedantists and the Brahmos. The Muslims and

Christians will realize him too. All will certainly realize God if they are earnest and sincere. Some people indulge in quarrels, saying "one cannot achieve anything unless one worships our Krishna" or "Nothing can be gained without the worship of Kali, our Divine Mother" or "One cannot be saved without accepting the Christian religion". This is pure dogmatism.'

It is in this deep and fundamental rejection of dogmatism by Sri Ramakrishna, his spiritual and temporal heir Swami Vivekananda, the monks of the Ramakrishna Order he founded and contemporary masters such as His Holiness The Dalai Lama whose influence continues to grow amongst millions in India and around the world, that we can find hope for our fractured and fragmented world.

Swami Vivekananda, recalling the message of his master, said: 'One must learn to put oneself into another man's very soul . . . no one ever before in India became Christian and Muslim and Vaishnava by turns.' He went on to say: 'The idea of harmony of religions, the idea of universal acceptance, and universal tolerance, will be a great acquisition to civilization. Nay, no civilization can exist unless this idea enters into it. No civilization can grow unless fanaticism, bloodshed and brutality stop.'

When asked about the Buddha, Sri Ramakrishna said: '*Meditating and becoming one with pure intelligence is the Buddha*' and noted that because the Buddha was unable to articulate and put into words the experience of his enlightenment he opted to be agnostic. Swami Vivekananda deeply immersed himself in Buddhism. In his vision the Buddha was the quintessential 'karma yogi'. Of him he said: '*I am the servant of the servants, of the servants of the Buddha. Who was there ever like Him? The Lord Buddha is my Ishta – my God. He preached no theory about Godhead – he was himself God, I fully believe it.*'

It has remained one of the great joys of my life that the teachings of both my teachers honour the many paths to human happiness and believe in the pre-eminence of the path of service, of serving others. The monks of the Ramakrishna Mission to this day embody the highest aspirations of the Buddhist ideal of the Bodhisattva who seeks enlightenment to teach and serve humanity. When His Holiness The Dalai Lama visited Belur Math, the headquarters of the Ramakrishna Mission, the two great teachers representing their great traditions struck an immediate rapport. They were to meet several times with deep affection and great mutual respect, including over a memorable public dialogue I was privileged to moderate.

What drew me first to the story of Sri Ramakrishna, as with that of the Buddha, was the willing, open acknowledgement and documentation of the sadhanas, the techniques, the practices and the struggles on the spiritual path. It offers us the reassurance and the opportunity to learn from their lives, that with the right motivation and right effort we too can arrive at similar realizations that will bring real, enduring freedom from suffering.

Though legend has it that there were celestial portents of the imminent birth of both and while many saw the sparks of the divine in the young Buddha and the young Ramakrishna, neither was spared the effort, the striving nor the pain, the suffering and the agonies of the journey from ignorance to the wisdom that brings final liberation. There was no divine or supernatural intervention that spared them a human sadhana. There was no spontaneous, cataclysmic effortless moment of truth that might suggest that their journeys were any easier or more comfortable than ours might be today. With the right motivation and the right effort their achievements can be ours.

If the Buddha and Sri Ramakrishna were to meet, while there is much they might see differently, they would bow to each other with humility and respect out of a knowing that the experiences of transformation by processes other than from one's own tradition can only enrich, not threaten, us.

Knowing that the lives of the great masters – Jesus, the Buddha, Muhammad, Sri Ramakrishna, Swami Vivekananda, The Dalai Lama – evolved from deep suffering to profound insights that inevitably led to an equanimity in which the otherness of the other dissolved, breeds a deep humility, a true celebration of diversity and plurality. While Ramakrishna publicly engaged in the sadhanas of other faiths, the Buddha experimented with the range of techniques and practices of his times before arriving at his own truths. Neither claimed they had created or transmitted something new, only that they had pierced the veils of ignorance to arrive at insights and techniques that could help others in their quest. This book is a humble offering about Sri Ramakrishna's quest.

May any merit gained from this effort help all sentient beings to find an end to their suffering.

— **Rajiv Mehrotra**

Introduction

O my mind, let us go home –
Why do you roam?
The earth, that foreign land
And wear its alien garb?
These senses, these elements
Are strangers; none is your own . . .
Why do you forget yourself
Falling in love with strangers?
O my mind, why do you

Kamarpukur village

$\mathcal{U}$nder the hurried exterior of modern India there is still a yearning for the eternal that has been the core of its existence for thousands of years. The sages of India accepted the reality of God as absolute fact, developing customs and rituals to enable ordinary men and women to attain the 'superconscious' in a natural way in the course of their daily lives. Of all the people of India, perhaps few are as intensely passionate as those of Bengal. Here, volatile emotions entwined with intense religious fervour create a special strain of ecstatic devotion that lies dormant, coiled under the soil, awaiting an exuberant release, sparked by a birth, a death, an event or an awakening. For centuries, Bengal has been the cradle of poets and revolutionaries, iconoclasts and free thinkers – and the fervent legions of God. Like the celebrated Bauls, or Sri Chaitanya, hailed as a reincarnation of Lord Krishna, dancing in spiritual rapture down dusty rural lanes, sparking off an incendiary wave of spiritual fervour from the Himalayas to the southern Cape, in the fifteenth century.

The spiritual culture of India has been resilient. The land has been inhabited for more than four thousand years by people whose heroes have not been kings, generals or politicians, but the solitary spirits who lived in caves, on the banks of rivers, on the summits of glaciers, meditating on the nature of existence, right behaviour or on virtue. Searching for the spark of the divine deep within their souls that tells man from beast, that is the dharma of humanity, the core of man's existence.

The culture of India was not a series of realities verified in laboratories that manipulated matter, but rare blooms of intuition proven in the delicate flowers of the mind, with roots in the invisible reaches of the spirit. India watched while Egypt, Greece and Persia flared like meteors across the skies in the cycles of civilization . . . .

Waves of conquerors came down into her fertile lap through the Himalayan passes – Sycthians, Parthians, Greeks, Huns, Mongols and Mughals. Yet when the last Mughal Emperor left the Red Fort in Delhi, after three centuries of political domination, the people of India remained committed to Sanatan Dharma – the eternal way of the ancient sages. Like a willow bending to the wind, the mind of India endured.

But, by the mid-nineteenth century, the start of the modern age, a storm of the spirit, brewing for centuries in Europe, began to spread its shadow over the world's ancient cultures. European scepticism and rationalist dogma, born out of the philosophies of the Age of Enlightenment and of Reason, analysed and divided, controlled and dominated, and removed the spirit from its sheath of matter. Religion in Europe had been intolerant and self-righteous. It had resulted in wars, it had been manipulated for political ends and bigoted priests stood in the way of further investigations into the secrets of nature. Religion must be separated from the State. The new European values that made quantum leaps in the domination of the environment for the comfort of man, rejected as myth and superstition anything too subtle to be grasped by the inflexible instruments of logical and rational thought.

India seemed the most vulnerable of all traditional societies to this new practicality, for how could a culture rooted in the spirit for four thousand years survive hurricanes of cold, hard facts that crushed truths too subtle for its grasp?

Western body-consciousness accepted as real only that which could be investigated through the five senses. The European mind turned outwards. Worldly enjoyment became the goal of life on earth. And as the West impacted on India, she lost her way to both enjoyment and liberation.

And indeed in Calcutta, the turbulent capital of a passionate land, young men reeled under the first intoxicating blizzard of European ideas, rumbling like juggernauts through the landscapes of the mind. Young men, who might have in an earlier age, turned their genius to the study and practice of their orthodox religions, began to believe that the European mind that augmented the individual, that had the power of impact on matter, the likes of which humanity had not witnessed before, was the way of the future.

Vying with their British masters, young Bengali intellectuals heaped scorn on their ancestors: India was backward, mired in superstition. India was asleep. The future was in the realm of matter, in the manipulation of matter and in the enquiry into matter. The new gods were Science and Standard of Living.

Science laughed at the gods. The gods, it appeared, must be banished. This was progress and India must awaken to the brave new world and keep in step with the rest of humanity. This was a judgement that reverberated across and down the century!

But unknown to the world, eighty-six miles northwest of Calcutta, in the Hooghly district, in the mud and thatch hamlet of Kamarpukur – dotted with little shrines, revelling in a healthy joyousness, in an environment not yet degraded by the onslaught of industrialization and malaria, around religious festivals and performances of sacred plays, crafts and harvests – the spiritual soul of India was preparing its response.

From out of this humble village hut came one of the greatest explorers of the inner realms that the world has known. A man who charted, with scientific precision in the laboratory of his own soul, each one of the ancient sadhanas – the paths which sages of yore had devised in their single-minded quest for God.

He traced each path to its goal and carefully mapped each obstacle, every cliff and chasm, each river and path, and every bend along the way. Then, when his search was complete, he shared with all those who would listen, the knowledge he had gained, and revealed to them the hidden purpose behind every ritual and myth in the Hindu tradition, and those in Islam and Christianity, in a manner that even the sceptic could accept.

For he did not quote from scriptures, or fall back on the mute authority of tradition, or retreat into the safety of dogma. He spoke from his own experience.

One

Birth, Childhood and Family

Why do you stand with your foot
on Hara's bosom mother?
With your tongue sticking out as though
you were just a simple girl?
O Saviour of the World,
I understand this hereditary trait –
Did not your mother too stand
on your father's bosom like this?

Rani Rasmani

*I*n all respects, Gadadhar was a normal, cheerful child, full of mischief and lively good humour. His spirited nature made him a pet of village mothers, and a favourite with playmates. Who could have seen the shape that young Gadadhar's future would take?

The creation of legends is a natural mark of human reverence for what one feels to be greater than oneself. Legends accumulate embellishments with the passing of generations, as well-intentioned historians repeat stories with their own additions. But legends take time to grow and Gadadhar was born less than 200 years ago – not time enough for legends. So what is related here could simply be fables. But it is important to remember that fables have their own truth.

At the age of fifty-one, Kshudiram Chattopadhyay thought he was too old to have a child, when, on a visit to a neighbouring village, he stopped to rest under the shade of a tree. Lord Rama, Kshudiram later reported, came to him in a dream, in the form of a celestial boy as green as a blade of *durva* grass. He pointed to the ground some distance away, and said: 'I have been lying here, neglected and starving for many days. Take me back to your house and serve me.' He refused to listen to the protests made by Kshudiram about his humble status.

On waking up, Kshudiram found a stone exactly at the spot Lord Rama had indicated in his dream. It was the *Shalagram* stone, an emblem of Lord Vishnu, the preserver of the universe, who comes to earth in this reincarnation – as dharma, virtue – when adharma, vice, threatens the world.

Kshudiram, a Rama bhakta, a worshipper of Lord Rama, hurried home with it and placed it in the household shrine. Nine years later, on a pilgrimage to Gaya to make offerings to departed ancestors at the temple of Gadadhar – another name for Lord Vishnu – Kshudiram had another dream. While his ancestors partook of Kshudiram's offerings, a divine effulgence appeared, seated on a throne, and told him he would come to earth as Kshudiram's son. Again, Kshudiram's protestations about his humble circumstances were brushed aside. At the same time, in Kamarpukur, Kshudiram's wife, Chandra Devi, a guileless and simple woman, also had a divine visitation. One night, she reported later, a radiant light in the exact form of her husband appeared beside her – and remained with her through the next day.

Chandra Devi later said:

All of a sudden, the image of Shiva came alive. The most beautiful light began to come from it. Waves of light filled the space around it. It came towards me and swallowed me up. I felt the light enter my body. And I fell down in a faint. When I returned to consciousness, I told Dhani what had happened. But she didn't believe me. She said it was an epileptic fit. But it was not so, because I felt so well. I knew I was with a child.

Chandra Devi was forty-five at the time. Both Kshudiram and Chandra Devi feared ridicule, therefore they told no one of their experiences. The name Ram appeared in the names of many Rama bhaktas. Kshudiram's own name ended in Ram, his first child was called Ramkumar, his next, Rameshwar. The child of their dreams, visions and visitations was born on 18 February 1836 at 5.15 a.m. (Bengali calendar: 17 February) and they named him Ramakrishna. But throughout his childhood everybody called him Gadadhar – Vishnu, who carried the mace.

Similar spiritual experiences were recorded by parents of great souls such as Sri Ramachandra, Lord Krishna and Sri Chaitanya. Whatever we may believe about the immaculate conception of Sri Ramakrishna – a remarkable parallel to the birth of Lord Buddha or Jesus Christ – Gadadhar appeared a normal boy, charming, naive and endearing. But he was without the drive and self-assured brilliance that usually marked out the ambitious, destined to forge their names in the world.

He was intelligent and gifted with a sharp retentive memory, but stubbornly opposed to abstractions such as mathematics that did not appeal to his poetic soul. He was an obedient child and well mannered up to a point; he was also strong-willed. Gadai, as he was lovingly called, rebelled against regimentation and rote memorization. Even as a child he seemed to understand the difference between the conventional knowledge of the schoolmaster and the wisdom of the soul. 'What use is an education,' he said, 'that teaches you only to bundle rice in a plantain leaf' (a priestly educational practice that helps one earn one's 'bread').

All the while during those sylvan years, Gadadhar's body and mind were being prepared from within for the awesome transformations that were to thrust him into terrifying, unknown, unlimited inner spaces, into which most feared to delve. The process was so subterranean as to be almost invisible to those around him.

However, every now and then, a glimpse of something colossal crashed briefly through the outer personality of the child, which would break the surface like a great whale from the deepest oceans of the soul. As Sri Ramakrishna later said, it was the magnificence of the contrast between the white cranes and the dark clouds that had overwhelmed him. His spirit, he later described, flew up towards the cranes and clouds, and his body fell unconscious. No one could have known at the time that he had attained his first spontaneous samadhi, a state of superconsciousness unknown to the mere mortal, but well-documented by the sages of the past. He was only six years old at that time.

This incident was repeated a few years later on a pilgrimage to the Vishalakshi shrine at Anur, a couple of miles north of Kamarpukur, where he was taken along by village women who enjoyed listening to the young Gadai sing. While singing a hymn in praise of the Goddess, Gadai fell unconscious. It was a small forewarning of the stormy years of awakening which were to come later – when Sri Ramakrishna as the priest of Kali, spent days balanced on the borderline of rapture. The least pretext – a strain of music, a divine name, a familiar face – became a window for his trembling spirit to pass into the luminescence of the inner world.

The close relatives of the boy who came to be known as Sri Ramakrishna Paramahamsa, the Great Swan, came with their own share of spiritual power. Sri Ramakrishna said of his father, in later years:

> My father spent most of his time in worship and meditation. While he was praying, his chest swelled and shone with a divine radiance, and tears rolled down his cheeks. The villagers stepped aside as he passed, they respected him as a sage.'

Everyone, young or old, was always welcome at Kshudiram's cottage, that despite poverty and suffering ever radiated a wonderful peace and joy.

The death of his father catalysed in Gadadhar a dispassion that bordered on depression. But where other children might have retreated into dumb unreasoning grief, Gadadhar became thoughtful. It was as though he saw clearly, for an instant, the transitory nature of life. His father's death transformed Gadai. He became serious and childhood games lost their former appeal. Sri Ramakrishna later recounted how much he wanted to take the begging bowl and join the itinerant monks. But he did not follow that path for fear that it would have broken his mother's heart.

As time flew by, Gadadhar began to show signs of unusual sagacity. Saints of many religions often show extraordinary wisdom from an early age. At a special ceremony in the midst of a heated argument amongst wise men, eleven-year-old Gadadhar stopped the free flow of philosophical hot air with a few succinct words! For the rest of that night he found himself in a strange and exalted realm where he could not be reached and none could follow. Thereafter, Gadadhar's spontaneous flights of spirit became more frequent. The divinity struggling to be born within the boy stirred intermittently. And each time it awakened, the umbilical cord that tied Gadadhar to the world of appearances loosened its hold.

Kshudiram was an exceptionally principled man. Originally from Dere, two miles west of Kamarpukur, he had been forced off his ancestral lands with his wife and two children, ruined by a tyrannical landowner who wanted him to bear false witness against a tenant. To Kshudiram, character counted more than cash. Fortunately a friend and benefactor, Sukhlal Goswami, ensured that the Chattopadhyay family had a reasonably comfortable life in Kamarpukur. On Kshudiram's death, however, the family entered times of privation. The eldest son Ramkumar, a Sanskrit scholar of repute, thereafter, provided for the family.

Ramkumar's wife died after giving birth to their son Akshay. He was unable to remain in Kamarpukur and needed a change of place while continuing to support his family. Ramkumar left for Calcutta to start a Sanskrit school.

The pressure on Gadai to earn a living increased – but to Gadai, school was not only irrelevant, it was something shameful. The thought of training his mind for skills required to accumulate wealth and worldly honours made him shudder with revulsion. The mind, he said, was created for higher things

– to realize God. Yet, even in the midst of sorrow there was time for that particular honesty of childhood that lays bare the pompous hypocrisy of the justifying adult mind.

A conservative neighbour, the trader Durgadas Pyne, often boasted that no male had ever penetrated his women's quarters, so strict was his family's adherence to purdah. Yet, Ramakrishna found a way to enter this restricted area where no one was able to guess who he really was till he revealed himself! All this time his mother was anxiously searching for him just as Lord Krishna's mother was regularly forced to find her mischievous son. The story goes:

Once the boy Krishna, up to his innumerable pranks, disappeared. Yasodha, his mother, was frantic with worry. A friend asked her, reasonably enough:

Why do you worry about the boy? He is after all, the Lord. He will look after himself. Yasodha's tart reply was: What Lord! It's my *son* I worry about.

It is part of our humanity to forget. So, stories of his divine origins notwithstanding, his family had not yet properly understood the passion for renunciation burning in young Gadadhar. Ramkumar felt his youngest brother was over indulged, that he was frittering away the best years of his life singing, modelling clay and playacting. A decision was arrived at and Gadai was sent to Calcutta to study with Ramkumar's other pupils, while he was also supposed to assist him as best he could.

Unknown to all, once Gadai left the timelessness and safety of village life for the anxious hurry and stumble of the city, Gadai's special destiny beckoned him faster – one that demonstrated to the modern world, the absolute necessity of ancient values for its health; that would juxtapose the new with the old.

The British were still traders – wealthy traders with armies and incipient governments. They grew more powerful each year, as the European mind perfected its technological impact on the world of matter. While living in the City of Palaces, an imposing European quarter in Calcutta, they held themselves in superior isolation from the largely subservient 'idol worshipping heathen', as they called those belonging to the land.

Widow of the enormously wealthy merchant Rajchandra Das, Rani (a maternal pet name; she was not a member of royalty) was widely respected for her shrewdness, generosity, courage and piety. At forty-four, she had already defeated a British attempt to tax fish caught on the River Hooghly. Facing ruin, local fishermen had approached Rani for redress. She bought the monopoly on fishing rights on the Ganga. The British were pleased to sell them to her – as they would tax her canneries. But Rani strung chains across the river to hold up British ships, claiming that shipping frightened the fish and therefore interfered with her rights! Of course, she would give up if the tax on fish was repealed. It was!

Dakshineswar temple, which was to become the home of young Gadai, was the dream of Rani Rasmani, a devotee of the Goddess Kali. Construction had begun in 1847 on 20 acres, partly bought from an Englishman, partly an old Muslim burial ground shaped like the back of a tortoise, which was said in the tantras to be conducive to the worship of Shakti. It took eight years to complete the temple at a cost of nine hundred thousand rupees.

However, close to completion, Rani came up against a major hurdle – she was born a *Kaivarta*, in a family of fishermen, considered by Brahmins to be of low caste. Therefore, no Brahmin agreed to officiate at her temple!

Until, when consulted, Ramkumar Chattopadhyay, who had by then earned a formidable reputation in Calcutta for his wisdom, learning and foresight, found an equitable solution: the temple was consecrated in the name of Rani Rasmani's guru who was a Brahmin.

On 31 May 1855, at considerable expense and amidst great festivities, the image of Kali was installed at Dakshineswar.

Formally called Sri Sri Jagadiswari Mahakali, the image is popularly known as Bhavatarini, meaning *She who takes Her devotees across the ocean of existence*. Many professors of the shastras and Brahmins came from distant centres of learning. The Rani was delighted when Ramkumar agreed to be the officiating priest of the Kali temple, on a temporary basis, because his school was not doing as well as he had hoped.

Gadai was eighteen at the time, and while sagacious, given to mystic experiences and accomplished in religious rituals (if not in mathematics), learned willingly at his brother's school. He was not yet the sagacious Sri Ramakrishna whom the world would revere. Gadai objected to moving to Dakshineswar, and to Ramkumar officiating at a temple constructed by a low-caste woman, no matter how wealthy.

He refused to move with his brother to the temple that was to be his home for the next twenty years – that was to be the safe cradle from which he would undertake his intense mystical journeys. So much so that his brother had to take recourse to the *dharmapatra* – the leaf of impartiality – a method popular in villages, of making the right decisions. 'Yes' and 'No' are written on *vilva* leaves placed in a pot. A child is then asked to pick one. Gadadhar pulled out the 'Yes'. God had made his wishes known, Gadai had to move. Yet, once at Dakshineswar he insisted on cooking his own meals.

Caste is today considered an unmitigated evil. But to understand Gadai's objections, one must understand the true nature of caste. The ancient sages started with the fundamental perception that men are *not* created equal. It was not a value judgement; merely a recognition of the fact that human beings were created with vastly different abilities. Human society was likened to a body. To ask the heart to do the work of the lungs was surely foolishness! Or ask the feet to do the work of the brain. Therefore, each individual must live by his dharma – the God-given law of his nature.

At the dawn of Indian civilization, the caste a man belonged to was determined by his occupation. By the sixth century BC, unfortunately, as is so often the case in human affairs, the fundamentals had been forgotten, conceptual reversals became the air men breathed – and the work a man did had begun to be determined by his caste.

Yet, as we have seen in the case of Rani Rasmani, caste was no barrier to attaining both material and spiritual fruit. In Gadai's orthodox family, caste was considered as natural a phenomenon and as little to be discussed as the monsoon or the rising of the sun. In objecting to Rani Rasmani, Gadai, who had insisted on the lower-caste Dhani giving him his first *bhiksha* at his sacred thread ceremony because he had said he would, was now challenged by the transgression not of a repressive hierarchy but the transgression of the divinely ordained nature of things. The time was yet to come when he would transcend all caste boundaries in his quest for union with the Absolute.

If Gadadhar was not yet fully the sage he would become, he was yet a poet with limitless resources of childlike wonder. He was naturally open to the daily rituals of a vibrant temple culture, to the spiritual potency of the sacred Ganga replete with the memories and myths of the race; the sacred river that had sprung from the matted locks of Lord Shiva. His distance from Dakshineswar could not last.

It is often said that when an intimate and lasting relationship of love is forged, the attraction leading to it is felt at first sight. The scriptures say this is a carryover from previous lives. Mathurnath Biswas, Rani's son-in-law, was a man of the world, a bejewelled, swaggering dandy with a keen business sense, hardly the kind of man to have been attracted to a priest. But below the man of the world lay a sincere devotion to the Divine Mother.

This devotion drew him to Gadai and enabled him to recognize in the boy that special quality, that spark that would erupt like a volcano of spiritual splendour in the years to come.

Mathur wanted Gadai to take over the puja in the temple but he was reluctant to do so. Just then Gadai's nephew, Hridayram, who was to become his closest companion and protector, arrived from Kamarpukur. It was Hriday who cajoled and persuaded Gadai, till he acquiesced to Mathur's demand. He agreed to perform the rituals to the Goddess if Hriday would take over the care of the ornaments since Gadadhar had a natural aversion to gold, money, jewels.

One day, the priest of the Radhakanta temple accidentally dropped the image of Krishna on the floor, breaking one of its legs. The worship of an image with a broken limb was against the scriptures, therefore Rani was advised by the priests to install a new image. Rani suggested that a new image be made available for worship and, in the meantime, also asked for Sri Ramakrishna's opinion since she was fond of the image.

In response, Ramakrishna started singing:

Why do you stand with your foot on Hara's bosom mother?
With your tongue sticking out as though you were just a simple
girl?
O Saviour of the World, I understand this hereditary trait –
Did not your mother too stand on your father's bosom like this?

Then he smiled and asked quite reasonably: 'What if Rani's son-in-law had broken his leg? Would she throw him away? Or give him medical treatment?'

To this a devotee remarked that it was a deity's image that had broken.

Ramakrishna was very amused at this remark and replied: 'Ah! What a fine understanding. Can He, who is an indivisible whole, be broken?'

Two

The Quest of the Spirit

Why won't you grant my prayer?
I've been praying to you for so long.
I cannot go on without a glimpse of you Mother,
I would rather die.

Goddess Kali

*R*amkumar wanted Sri Ramakrishna to learn the intricate rituals involved in the worship of Kali. In order to become a priest of Kali, he had to be initiated by a qualified guru. A suitable Brahmin was found, but no sooner did his guru whisper a holy word in his ear, Ramakrishna, overwhelmed with emotion, uttered a loud cry and plunged into deep concentration that lasted for about five days.

Hriday, worried at his uncle's ways, interrupted him and said, 'Mama! You have gone without food and water for five days. You must eat. Every tree needs some water.'

Sri Ramakrishna felt disturbed, stirred from his deep concentration and replied, 'Hridu? Don't you know you must not disturb me when I am praying?'

At the young age of twenty, one foot in the door of priesthood, the young Ramakrishna heard that his brother Ramkumar, old before his time at fifty, had died on a visit to a village not far from Calcutta. It was the second time in his young life that Ramakrishna felt the chill wind of death on his skin. The effect was immediate and sobering. Behind the shimmering mirage of life surely something more permanent was concealed. The search to find that soon became the sole purpose of his life. He had not even skirted the edges of it yet.

Sri Ramakrishna's yearning for a living vision of the Mother intensified as he continued worshipping in the temple. He spent more and more time in meditation and chose an extremely solitary place for this purpose – in the midst of a dense jungle, thick with underbrush and prickly plants, which lay to the north of the temple. This place, used as a burial ground in the past, was shunned by people for fear of ghosts. Ramakrishna used to spend entire nights in meditation and return to his room with swollen eyes only in the morning.

Hriday was bewildered when he discovered that his uncle used to lay aside his cloth and his Brahminical thread while meditating. He reproached him, saying: 'Uncle, you are meditating without your sacred thread!'

Ramakrishna replied in a most composed manner:

The sacred thread symbolizes bondage; it says I am a Brahmin and therefore superior. We should be free from the eight bonds that tie us down.

Hriday was intrigued and questioned his uncle about the eight bonds. Sri Ramakrishna explained:

Hatred, fear, shame, aversion, egoism, vanity, pride of noble descent and obsession with formal good conduct are the eight bondages. When one calls on the Mother one should discard all bondages and seek with a concentrated mind.

In every possible sense, Ramakrishna's assumption of the priesthood of Kali was the watershed event in his life. The resolve to dedicate himself to God remained essentially formless and unfocussed until then. The image of Kali, around which his priestly day revolved, acted as a powerful lens to focus his scattered yearning to the point of a flame. And the spirit that soon burned with a ferocious intensity of devotion that had hardly been equalled in human history began to coalesce.

In the religious history of the world, except for scattered incidents, no detailed account is available of the spiritual disciplines and practices of those aspiring to unite with God. No details are known of the alternating waves of pain and pleasure, hope and despair suffered in their indomitable search. No connections are traceable between the incidents of childhood and wondrous actions of a realized adult life.

However, one possible theory could be that devotees needed to suppress facts of human weakness not conducive to the lives of superhuman incarnations who should, they believed, at all times display perfect universal love and tolerance . . . But then, as Sri Ramakrishna said later, 'Shape cannot be given to an ornament of pure gold, it must contain some alloy.'

Yet, this was only a foretaste of the intense experiences to come. His first glimpse of the Divine Mother made him more eager for Her uninterrupted vision. He wanted to see Her both while he was meditating deeply and with eyes open. But he felt that the Mother was playing a game of hide and seek with him which intensified both his joy and suffering. While he wept bitterly when he was separated from Her, he used to fall into a trance and cheer up immensely when he found Her again. During this period of spiritual practice he underwent many uncommon experiences. When he sat to meditate, he could hear strange clicking sounds in the joints of his legs, as if someone were locking his meditation. He heard the same sounds again, this time unlocking them and leaving him free to move about. He also saw flashes floating before his eyes, or a sea of deep mist with luminous waves around him.

At times he beheld the Mother rising from a sea of translucent mist and felt Her breath and heard Her voice. While worshipping in the temple he sometimes became exalted, sometimes remained as motionless as a stone and sometimes almost collapsed from excessive emotion. Many of his actions, contrary to all tradition, seemed sacrilegious to the devotees. Often, Ramakrishna took a flower and touched it to his own head, body and feet, and then offered it to the

Goddess. At other moments he sang to himself addressing the Divine Mother:

Here is thy knowledge Mother, and here is thy ignorance. Here is thy good, and here thy evil. Here is thy vice and here thy virtue. Here is thy fame and here thy calumny. Grant me pure devotion at thy lotus feet and show thyself to me. O Devi, pure Consciousness, manifested in all sciences from which endless forms of conceptual knowledge arise. You exist as all female forms of the world; you alone pervade the universe. You are incomparable and beyond words. Who can describe your numberless qualities merely by reciting hymns to you?

This seemingly bizarre behaviour caused immense turmoil in the minds of the devotees. While some called him mad, some were of the opinion that he was possessed and yet others thought his behaviour absolutely blasphemous.

One day Sri Ramakrishna fed a cat the food that was to be offered to Kali. This was too much for the manager of the temple garden, who considered himself responsible for the proper conduct of worship. He immediately reported Ramakrishna's insane behaviour to Mathur Babu.

Sri Ramakrishna later described the incident:

The Divine Mother revealed to me in the Kali temple that it was She who had become everything. She showed me that everything was full of consciousness – the image, the altar, and even the marble floor was Consciousness. I found everything inside the room soaked as it were, in bliss – the Bliss of God. I saw a wicked man in front of the Kali temple; but in him also I saw the power of the Divine Mother vibrating. That is why I fed a cat with the food that was to be offered to the Divine Mother. I clearly perceived that the

Divine Mother was to be found everywhere and in everything – even the cat. Although the manager of the temple garden wrote to Mathur Babu, complaining that I fed the cat with the offering intended for the Mother, Mathur Babu had an insight into the state of my mind. Therefore, he wrote back to the manager saying: 'Let him do whatever he likes. You must not say anything to him. He is in sadhana. It seems he will awaken the spirit of the Mother in her stone image. The installation of Devi has answered its purpose.'

This controversial priest of Kali, whose behaviour was almost beyond human comprehension, had, unknown even to himself, since he had no teachers to guide him, entered a new phase of his life, one characterized by what Hindus call sadhana, Christians call the mystic union and Buddhists call nirvana.

It is said there are two paths to sadhana: the path of discrimination and the path of devotion. Discrimination is rational – it thinks, it rejects things that are impermanent, *neti, neti, neti* (not this): I am not my house, I am not my money, I am not my body, I am not my mind . . . until by a process of elimination the aspirant comes to that which is permanent and therefore, real. The path of knowledge has a concept of the Ultimate Ideal from the beginning, and goes forward consciously towards it.

The devotee, on the other hand, travels forward with faith, ignorant of where he will ultimately arrive. He accepts all: 'You are this and that and also this.' Thereby reminding himself that Brahman exists in all things. He does not worship the thing, but the Reality within the thing.

This was Ramakrishna's route.

A literal man, needing to experience everything himself, he was finding his own way, blundering through the dense undergrowth of his mind, the high altitudes of his soul. With unflinching faith and intense yearning he prayed to the Mother of the Universe for realization, surrendering himself totally to Her wishes. He took up various religious paths one after another and followed them faithfully. Having seen for himself the same goal at the end of every path, he one day declared: 'As many faiths so many paths.'

Very often, Ramakrishna, in his state of utter desperation, cried out to the Mother and said:

Yet another day gone by, Mother . . . what is life worth if I cannot see you?

I have suffered so long. Are you just a chunk of stone?

Or is there a divine Consciousness within? Ah Mother, sometimes I doubt you exist. Am I a fool to believe there exists a Consciousness of which this stone is only a representation? Mother, you have shown yourself to other devotees. Why won't you show yourself to me?

He would also plead:

Why won't you grant my prayer?
I've been praying to you for so long.
I cannot go on without a glimpse of you Mother,
I would rather die.

Three

Blundering

Towards the Divine

Lives there one who knows Kali, my Divine Mother?
The Consort of the Absolute, the Spirit of Eternity.
The six schools of philosophy cannot know her.

Mathurnath Biswas

$\mathcal{U}$p to this point Sri Ramakrishna's passions were recognizable on a human scale. We can sympathize with Gadadhar the truant, dream with Gadadhar the dreamer, empathize with Gadadhar the poet. We can identify with a young lad who rejects hypocrisy to forge his own way in the world. We can identify with a boy who emulates mythic heroes – we have done all this ourselves in our youth. We have been able to follow him through his sudden, inexplicable withdrawals from the material world with perplexity and some bemusement. But now the road turns precipitously, out of the gentle forest, climbs up steep inclines, falling into chasms, straining over jagged peaks – which the more normal amongst us are loath to tread. Identifying with a mature young man driven to conducting a frenzied pursuit of a stone goddess for years together is not easy.

Ramakrishna had seemingly come to the culmination of his 'dark night of the soul'. He described this experience later, thus:

Suddenly, I had a marvellous vision of the Mother. Then it was as if houses, doors, temples – everything vanished. And there was nothing. I saw an infinite shoreless sea of light, a sea that was Consciousness. However far and in whatever direction I looked, I saw shining waves coming towards me, raging and storming at great speed. Then they were on me and engulfed me and I sank into the depths of infinity.

There are similar descriptions in other cultures and other times, of mystics being 'flooded with light'. But in their deepest mind they have seen themselves as sparks of consciousness 'speeding towards the light'. They have 'seen the light' or 'entered the light'. And the experience has transformed them. On the material plane, saints are shown with halos of light.

However, this vision of the Mother, longed for and hungered after, was not sufficient to bring Sri Ramakrishna out of the shadows of eternity. While a lesser soul might bask comfortably in the afterglow of the radiance of one vision, Sri Ramakrishna's restless spirit could not be satisfied with one charmed interlude – that vanished, leaving in its wake only the hollow certainty of impermanence.

He accepted nothing short of an utter and continuous union with the permanent source of all things. He entertained only continuous bliss. Searching for this union, he entered a state he was himself later to term *unmada* or insanity, Godly madness.

Sri Ramakrishna constantly held conversations with the Mother and felt Her presence and talked as if to a child, 'Come Mother, eat. Or shall I eat first? Will that make you happy?' He then turned and fed a cat and said: 'Ah there you are! Ma, here, eat. Mother, you are in all things. Blessed are you, O Divine.' He sometimes also lay down with the statue of Kali and said, 'Mother, I will sleep by your side. For am I not your child?' He often felt Her face and chucked Her fondly under the chin. Once he even placed a finger under the nostril of the statue. 'Ah! yes, I feel you breathe. Are you breathing, Mother?' He became frenzied and wept and said, 'Mother, Mother, where are you. I've lost you, Mother.' And he began to beat the floor, roll around on it like a lost child. While continuing to weep, he banged his head on the floor and said, 'Mother, Mother, why have you left me again?'

Now Sri Ramakrishna saw the Mother often, suddenly, sporadically, in all things. Sometimes he saw Her and sometimes he lost Her. His search drove everyone at Dakshineswar to paroxysms of anxiety. Even the most pious visitors to the temple, accustomed to seeing a wide range in manifestations of religious fervour, found Sri Ramakrishna's behaviour nothing short of dementia.

During those intense moments he sang and sometimes improvised lines in composed songs like:

Lives there one who knows Kali, my Divine Mother?
The Consort of the Absolute, the Spirit of Eternity.
The six schools of philosophy cannot know Her
The Yogi meditates upon Her as Muladhara and Sahasrara
The Goose and the Gander mate in the lotus wilderness –
They are Eternity and His Consort, my Divine Mother
She who gives birth to the Universe – how great is
She who appears in all Her majesty in every finite being.
To think that one can know Her is to imagine one can
swim the mighty ocean
My mind knows this, but my heart will not see –
It is a dwarf that aspires to reach the moon.

Kali, of the terrifying blackness, of the lolling tongue and severed heads. Kali, with blood on her hands . . . Why, we must ask ourselves, would a young man of such extraordinary purity of character, such a fine spirit of renunciation, reach out with such deranged recklessness towards a black basalt image? What did the Goddess Kali symbolize to this 'Madman of God'?

The answer surely lies in a realm beyond earthly ties. In the realm of symbol and metaphor; in the human search for permanence, for meaning, in our all-too-temporary sojourn on earth.

Kali is the Universal Mother, the maternal mystery at the heart of our lives to which we are tied forever, by invisible but real umbilical cords. The darkness of deepest space out of which, without volition, we were born, and to which we must, without volition return. Our dependence on the mystery is absolute; our intimacy with this mystery is infinite. No human relationship can compare with it.

Kali, the embodiment of universal energy, *shakti*, the appalling power that makes and unmakes the universe. Kali of the two faces. Those who swim against Her laws, seeking false security in Her creations, see only Her horrific face, for She is Maya, the Mother of illusions. To them She is death, for all that is 'matter' to which they cling with such desperation, must be thrown into the cycle of birth and death.

To those who strive to unite with Her, flowing with the currents of the world, recognizing the pointlessness of clinging to things that must change, She shows Her benevolent face. It would not have occurred to our ancestors to doubt Her existence or to question the wisdom of dedicating the best energies of a lifetime in Her pursuit. But in a world dedicated to matter, we have become strangers to this Divine Mother. We have become strangers to ourselves. It takes a Sri Ramakrishna to remind us.

Once it so happened that when Sri Ramakrishna was performing a ritual, he began to shake uncontrollably and gradually became rigid and went into samadhi. Later, he explained his experience thus:

> I saw particles of light like swarms of fireflies. Sometimes light covered everything like a mist. At other times everything was pervaded with light like molten silver. I didn't understand what I was seeing. I didn't know whether it was good or bad. I just prayed: 'Mother, I don't understand what is happening to me. I don't know the scriptures or mantras. Please teach me how to know you. If you won't teach me, who will?'

At that time, the devotees of the temple were simply concerned and uncomfortable. And Sri Ramakrishna gave them enough cause.

One day Rani Rasmani walked into the inner sanctum of the Kali temple and saw Sri Ramakrishna in a state of bliss. Rani requested Sri Ramakrishna to sing a song on Kali:

Ramakrishna responded and sang:

> *Lives there one who knows Kali, my Divine Mother?*
> *The Consort of the Absolute, the Spirit of Eternity.*
> *The six schools of philosophy cannot know her.*

During that time Rani's attention wandered. Ramakrishna immediately felt this and reprimanded her saying, 'Shame on you! Thinking such thoughts at a time like this!'

The devotees were greatly baffled and angry at Sri Ramakrishna's act. Mathur begged him to keep his feelings under control in future and heed the conventions of society. Simultaneously, he chided the devotees and said, 'Be quiet. I'm sure the Bhattacharya has his reasons.' Rani supported his words and said:

Yes! He does. Instead of listening to the hymn, I was thinking about that lawsuit I'm involved in. I was enmeshed in worldliness when I should have been worshipping the Divine. It was not Baba, it was the Divine Mother herself who struck me and enlightened my heart.

The concern about Sri Ramakrishna's madness grew by the hour. Hriday kept asking himself if his uncle had gone mad. He was worried about his uncle's health and brought it to Mathur Babu's notice. He reported that his uncle had become very thin and hardly ever ate anything. His chest looked flushed. He bled from the very pores of his skin. 'What can I do?' he asked. Quite often, Sri Ramakrishna was found wandering across the courtyard to the temple, bedecked with flowers and sandal paste.

Then, suddenly, Sri Ramakrishna stopped performing rituals at the Kali temple. At the time the uninitiated found it hard to realize that as a man progressed on the path to spiritual development, his regular actions gradually fell from him. Religious rituals became unimportant. Now Sri Ramakrishna no longer needed the image of Ma Kali to focus his attention, to find a path to the Divine Radiance. He worshipped the Mother in all things.

Sri Ramakrishna's unconventional behaviour was a major point of discussion between Rani and Mathur Babu. Mathur told Rani that a part of him thought that Sri Ramakrishna was not only sane, but super sane. 'But,' he said, 'a part of me cannot help thinking that he has traces of insanity as well and he might be suffering from a nervous disorder.' When Rani heard this, she ordered Mathur to get the best Ayurveda doctor available. But Mathur, who had tried all the conventional approaches, replied: 'The doctor says there's nothing wrong with him. In fact, he has an amazingly strong constitution.' Mathur also narrated an incident when he had bought a shawl for him from Benares. Although Sri Ramakrishna initially admired the gift, he later threw it on the ground and trampled on it saying: 'It's nothing but goats' hair. A blanket is as good. Will owning such a beautiful thing help me realize God?'

Mathur Babu and Rani Rasmani began to ascribe the mental ailment of Sri Ramakrishna in part, at least, to his observance of rigid continence and practising a celibate life. Thinking that a natural life would relax his nerves, both Mathur Babu and Rani engineered a plan with two women of ill-repute. Both the women were sent to seduce Sri Ramakrishna.

When Sri Ramakrishna saw the women he exclaimed: 'Ah Divine Mother, how beautiful you are!' And went into samadhi.

Mathur realized what a fool he was and so did the women, who fell at the master's feet begging forgiveness.

What, we might ask, is this samadhi into which Sri Ramakrishna was falling. Can one ever become *achaitanya* (unconscious)? However, the difference is that the mystic not only retains affectionate ties to the world, he comes out of mystical retreat with new visions, deeper realizations, a greater integration of personality and an enhanced ability to make fine perceptual distinctions. The psychotic remains bound to his dead, dark world of attempted escape.

Samadhi, put simply, is the fourth state of consciousness, neither waking nor dreaming, nor a dreamless sleep. Only the merest handful of people in the world experience it, and those that do, find it difficult to describe; for the state of samadhi is by nature indescribable; words deal with knowledge obtained by the five senses; samadhi goes beyond the experience of senses.

While in samadhi, one transcends the ego. It is a state of awareness, unimaginably more intense than everyday consciousness. It is the very opposite of a trance; for trance is at the very least a condition of stupor or bewilderment. In his vision of Kali, Sri Ramakrishna had attained, unknown to himself and those around him, a level called *savikalpa* samadhi, the highest level within the realm of form. For, at this level he had attained the form of the Mother, to which he was deeply attached as if he were a child.

The psychic world, or that below the material, is experienced in dreams, under drugs and sometimes even when awake. These are psychic visions that can depress and terrify and are sometimes neutral. Psychic experiences remain attached to the world and do not change the individual. Beyond the psychic the mind loses awareness of the material world and enters the realm of the spiritual, always accompanied by feelings of great joy – for the devotee is then closer to the essential centre.

For anyone in a normal state of consciousness, Sri Ramakrishna's actions certainly seemed to be the mood swings of an utter maniac. But once again, below the surface was a serious intent. Yearning for the realization of his family deity – Raghubir, the Lord Rama, whom he had worshipped as a child – literal-minded Sri Ramakrishna immersed himself quite unknowingly in *dasa bhava*. He transformed himself into Lord Rama's greatest devotee, Hanuman, the monkey, the *dasa* or servant who followed his Lord's word without the slightest question, murmur or hesitation. Sri Ramakrishna was heard calling out, *Raghubir! Raghubir!* And it was later discovered that when Sri Ramakrishna meditated in Panchavati with his eyes open, Sita appeared to him in a nimbus of light. She smiled and moved towards Sri Ramakrishna, who cried out in recognition, *Mother!* He rose with hands folded while Mother Sita put her hands on his head and smiled and merged into him.

Sri Ramakrishna was not in samadhi at the time. During this intense phase of worship of Lord Rama, it was Sita whom he saw, who blessed him and passed into his body, making a gift to him of Her smile. Henceforth, Sri Ramakrishna's smile was said to be as sweet as that of Sita's.

Sri Ramakrishna's sadhanas, his long sessions in samadhi, were taking a toll on his mind and body while bringing him to priceless realizations about the nature of existence that he would begin to share with the world when the time came.

But life was not without its lighter moments. In 1858, Sri Ramakrishna's cousin Ramtarak Chattopadhyay, whom Ramakrishna called Haladhari, came to live in Dakshineswar, remaining there for about eight years. On account of Sri Ramakrishna's indifferent health, Mathur appointed Haladhari the official priest of the Kali temple. Though a scholarly Vaishnavite, well-versed in the scriptures, he was hardly aware of their spirit. Albeit devout, he was pompous, arrogant about his intellectual achievements and orthodoxy of Brahminhood.

Haladhari was a complex character. He loved to participate in hair-splitting theological discussions and, by the measure of his own erudition proceeded to gauge Sri Ramakrishna. An orthodox Brahmin, he thoroughly disapproved of his cousin's unorthodox actions, though he was not unimpressed by Sri Ramakrishna's purity of life, ecstatic love of God and yearning for realization.

Once, Haladhari affectionately and patronizingly addressed Sri Ramakrishna:

> Gadai, I do intensely disapprove of your throwing away your thread – do you believe you have reached such a high level of attainment that you can be so casual about caste rules? Yet . . . sometimes, I admit, I do catch a glimpse of the tremendous presence that has so mysteriously chosen to dwell in your emaciated body and half-crazed mind.

Sri Ramakrishna laughingly said, 'Are you sure? Then why do you not accept me as I am?' To which Haladhari replied, 'Sometimes I doubt you. For you break every rule of caste, and you are almost wholly uneducated.'

Becoming serious at Haladhari's words, Sri Ramakrishna asked, 'But now you are sure?'

Haladhari responded with syrupy sweetness, 'When I see the sweetness of your devotion, how can I be anything but sure? After all I am a priest, and I have some inner vision.' Sri Ramakrishna teasingly answered, 'Let's see how long your certainty lasts.'

Upon hearing this, Haladhari pompously narrated a Sanskrit quote and said, 'As it is said in the Adhyatma Ramayana . . .'

Cutting him short, Sri Ramakrishna observed, 'I already know all that. I have realized all the states you talk about. I know everything that's written in your scriptures.'

Haladhari was furious and said, 'You idiot! You uneducated fool. Do you think you can understand the scriptures?'

Offended, but with seriousness, Sri Ramakrishna answered, 'Believe me, brother, he who lives inside this body teaches me everything.'

Haladhari got even more furious and shouted, 'Get out of here, you crazy blockhead. Do you think you're an incarnation of Vishnu?'

Sri Ramakrishna sweetly and gently replied, 'But Dada, you said you were sure this time.' Usually, it was the simple Sri Ramakrishna who was at the receiving end of Haladhari's arrogant intellect and vast learning.

Once, when Sri Ramakrishna was coming out of the Kali temple, Haladhari intercepted him and derisively asked, 'How can you spend your time worshipping a *Tamasika* goddess who embodies nothing but destruction? It was the curse of Kali that killed my child.'

Sri Ramakrishna turned back to the temple with tears in his eyes and looking at the image of Kali, cried out, like an upset child, 'Mother! Haladhari who is a great scholar, says you are nothing but wrath and destruction. Can this be true?'

Later, while Haladhari sat in front of Krishna's image in the Radhakanta temple, Sri Ramakrishna came rushing in excited, jumped on Haladhari's back and said, 'Mother is everything! Do you dare call Her wrathful? No! She has every attribute, every quality – and yet She is nothing but pure love!'

Haladhari was shocked; his feelings underwent a radical change as his old feelings crumbled. He picked up some flowers and placed them on Sri Ramakrishna's feet saying, 'You touched me Master. You have touched me. I see. I see . . .'

Meanwhile, a garbled report of Sri Ramakrishna's failing health, indifference to worldly life and various abnormal activities reached Kamarpukur and filled his poor mother's heart with anguish. At her repeated requests, he returned to his village for a change of air. But his boyhood friends did not interest him any more. A divine fever consumed him. He spent a great part of the day and night in one of the cremation grounds, deep in meditation. The place reminded him of the impermanence of the human body, human hopes and achievements. It also reminded him of Kali, the Goddess of Destruction.

In the eighteenth century, in the days of Siraj-ud-Daulah, there lived in Bengal a man called Ram Prasad, famed and revered as the poet of the 'Motherhood of God'. He had written thus:

> *In the world's markets,*
> *the Mother flies her kites:*
> *souls soaring with winds,*
> *yearning to be free;*
> *held to the Earth*
> *with strands of illusion.*
> *In a hundred thousand*
> *She in the limitless sky,*
> *the kite wings up to the Infinite –*
> *see how gleefully She laughs*
> *and claps Her hands.*

Doubtless, Sri Ramakrishna too knew the thrill of free flight, the exhilaration of unfettered spaces and the terror of being cut loose from his social moorings; felt the vertigo of a soul freed from its familiar landscapes, perceiving the fathomless abyss below. Some part of him must have yearned for the more predictable, earthbound dullness of routine normalcy. For when his mother heard of his mad exertions at Dakshineswar, and called him home with the simple faith that the familiar surroundings of childhood would stabilize him, he came. Emaciated from his austerities, exhausted, he heaved a sigh of relief. He was twenty-four.

Sri Ramakrishna was welcomed by Rameshwar and Akshay.

His mother Chandra Devi and Dhani, his maid when he was a child, discussed the situation with each other. Chandra Devi felt that her son was going mad. He kept crying 'Mother! Mother!' Shocked at hearing this, Dhani said, 'He cried for you? A grown-up boy like that! Now that he's home you can give him the comfort he needs.'

Chandra Devi smiled ruefully and said, 'Ah, my friend, I am not the Mother he longs for. I wish it were that simple.'

Perplexed, Dhani enquired, 'Where is he now?'

Rameshwar replied that he was meditating in the Bhutirkhal, under the peepul tree, while the jackals howled around him.

Shocked, Dhani asked, 'But why? Why in the cemetery with all the dead!'

Akshay and Rameshwar informed her that that's where the Mother he was seeking was likely to be found. Cemeteries are the ultimate symbol of impermanence.

Even more worried, Dhani said, 'That doesn't sound right. It's a lonely place. He might do himself harm. He's not well.' To which Chandra Devi said the *vaidya* had assured her that her son was healthy. The exorcist never found him possessed by any spirit, and he had no disease.

Chandra Devi was almost sure that her son had gone mad and he must be saved before the desire for Kali possessed him again. At this point, Dhani suggested that Ramakrishna should get married and everybody agreed.

The very thought of marriage is usually anathema for those drawn to a life of the spirit. For the conservative and family-centred occupations of marriage cast a cold chill on the spiritual idealism of youth. Shuttered behind the walls of attachment and worldly care, the life of a householder is truly bondage. An inhibition of the spirit: *samsara*. Yet, Sri Ramakrishna, in the midst of a storm of renunciation, was surprisingly delighted at the idea.

However, when the search began for a suitable girl, it was frustrating at every turn. Unmarried girls of the right age, disposition and family background were hard to find. And when a prospective match was located, the demands made on Chandra Devi and Rameshwar fell beyond their limited means. Till Sri Ramakrishna, in a meditative state, himself pointed the way.

Watching his mother and Rameshwar going from pillar to post, consulting different matchmakers with no positive achievement, he told them: 'There's no point running here and there. Go to the house of Ram Mukhopadhyay in the village of Jayarambati. The bride has been marked with straw and kept reserved for me.'

In Bengal it was customary to put aside the finest fruit and vegetable as an offering to God. These were tied with a straw around the stem to mark them out from those due for the market. Sarada was indeed, as it will be seen, an offering to God.

Sri Ramakrishna's marriage to Saradamani Devi was not destined to be a conventional one. When she attained puberty he did not become her conjugal husband but a spiritual guide, who prepared her to carry his work forward after his death. In his unusual relationship with Sarada, Sri Ramakrishna demonstrated that beyond the satisfaction of the senses, there is a higher purpose to marriage. With the insights of spiritual attainment, he knew this when he pointed out the place and family unseen, a girl who at the time was five years old and lived the next ten years with his mother. The matchmaker, he said, was the Divine Mother Herself.

Sri Ramakrishna spent one year and seven months at Kamarpukur, cherished by those who knew him. He rested and recovered the energies he had depleted in spiritual disciplines. Then, as Chandra Devi had feared, the call from the Divine Mother became too strong for him to resist. He left his child bride with his mother and returned to Dakshineswar.

In the Dakshineswar temple, Sri Ramakrishna got back to his old routine with more vigour, and the brief idyll of restful peace was shattered. He began his sadhanas without taking care of his physical self. The 'Godly madness' with its terrible physical symptoms appeared again, this time even more intensely. He spent days in the Panchavati meditating under the scorching sun and late into the nights. One day to the next, one hour to the next, Sri Ramakrishna was tossed from vision to despair and back again. All thoughts of brother, mother and bride disappeared from his mind.

His physical self deteriorated. His hair became so matted that birds sat on his head. But he paid no attention to these irritants. He was found weeping or rubbing his face on the ground or sitting up imploring the sky in the harsh sunlight. Hriday, his devoted nephew, carried food to him and generally looked after his physical body as best as he could.

Recalling this period, Sri Ramakrishna later remarked:

It was like being in the midst of a whirlwind – even my sacred thread was blown away. Sometimes I would open my mouth and it would be as if my jaws reached from heaven to the underworld. I felt I had to pull the Mother in towards me as a fisherman pulls in a fish.

He further explained:

Sometimes I shared my food with a dog. I had no sleep for six long years; my eyes lost the power of blinking. I tried to close my eyelids with my finger and I couldn't. I thought: I am on the verge of insanity. I cried out: 'Mother is this what happens to those who call on you? I surrender myself to you and you give me this terrible disease?' I wept. The next moment I was filled with ecstasy. And my body didn't matter. 'Let my body go, Mother,' I cried. 'It does not matter, but do not forsake me.' Mother appeared to me and comforted me.

His body trembled and burned. The pain began at sunrise and by midday it was unbearable. To ease the burning, Sri Ramakrishna stood in the Ganga with a wet towel on his head for two to three hours. Had it not been for Hriday, his constant companion, Sri Ramakrishna might have died. It was at this time that Sri Ramakrishna and Hriday planted a grove of five holy trees that came to be known as the Panchavati: fig, amalaki, banyan, asoka and bilva for the purposes of Sri Ramakrishna's austerities.

Days passed by in the same manner with Sri Ramakrishna's unconventional behaviour increasing every hour and once he was even seen in the Shiva temple reciting the *Mahima Stotra*:

With the blue mountain for ink,
A branch of the heaven tree as a pen,
And all the Earth as her writing leaf,
Were the goddess Sarada to describe your greatness
She could not – though she were to write forever.

Ramakrishna, in his state of seeming madness, cried out:

Oh great Lord God, how can I express your glory! Oh great Lord God, how can I express your glory! Oh great Lord God, how can I express your glory! Oh great Lord God, how can I express your glory! Oh great Lord God, how can I express your glory?

A passer-by thought he was crazier than usual and feared that in a moment he would ride on Shiva's shoulder, so he called out to Mathur to remove this madman. Mathur threatened the devotees that he would take them to task if they so much as touched Sri Ramakrishna. By then Sri Ramakrishna recovered and naively asked if he had done anything wrong. Mathur assured him and said, 'Oh no, Master! You were just reciting a hymn and I came to see that no one interrupted you.'

Once Mathur looked out of the window and watched Sri Ramakrishna pacing around in the distance. Suddenly Mathur ran, fell at Sri Ramakrishna's feet and wept inconsolably. Shocked at Mathur's behaviour, Sri Ramakrishna said, 'Babu what are you doing? You're a gentleman and Rani's son-in-law! What will people say if they see you acting like this? Calm yourself. Please. Get up!'

Mathur, unable to control himself said, 'Baba, I was watching you walk up and down. And I saw it distinctly. As you came towards me, you became Ma Kali. As you walked away, you became Lord Shiva. I couldn't believe my eyes. I rubbed them. But it happened again.'

Sri Ramakrishna looked disturbed and said, 'What are you saying, Mathur Babu? You are not well. Don't go around saying such things, people will say I've put a spell on you.'

Mythologizing? Creating legends? The truth? Whose truth? It's difficult to say. Suffice that Mathur was rewarded for his implicit and unshakeable belief in Sri Ramakrishna.

Thus far Sri Ramakrishna had only the internal evidence of his visions to support their authenticity. And he did not have the scriptural knowledge to allay his own doubts. What the young priest needed was an independent judgement from someone with the breadth of vision and training to verify his experiences. But where could such enlightenment be found? He was surrounded by people to whom he was a mystery – including Mathur and Rani for whom he was wondrous and holy, but a mystery nevertheless. Then, Rani Rasmani died with a vision of Mother Kali before her eyes. Sadly, her eldest daughter Padma also died without signing the deed handing over control of the temple.

In the deepest reaches of his being, Sri Ramakrishna was alone and exposed; he ploughed ahead in uncharted seas by sheer instinct, without even a map.

Four

1860

O auspiciousness of all auspicious things.
O door of all actions.
O refuge.
Three-eyed-one.
O spouse of Shiva,
O Narayani.
I bow down to thee.
I bow down to thee.

Panchavati

*O*ne day while Sri Ramakrishna was in the garden picking flowers, a boat pulled up at the Bakulghat embankment and a Bhairavi stepped out.

Sri Ramakrishna hurried to Hriday and with excitement said, 'There is a Brahmani who has stepped out of a boat at the ghat. Ask her to come to me.'

Hriday was perturbed, 'Master, a woman? You want me to bring a woman to you? Who is she? Does she know you? Why should she come?'

Sri Ramakrishna, unable to conceal his tears, replied, 'O Hridu. This is no ordinary woman. Something tells me she has been sent to me. Tell her Sri Ramakrishna asks for her. And she will come.'

Hriday followed the order and brought the Bhairavi to Sri Ramakrishna. Excited and happy, she seemed to recognize Sri Ramakrishna and said, 'Ah my child! Here you are at last. I knew you lived on the banks of the Ganga. I've been searching for you so long.'

To which Sri Ramakrishna shyly asked, 'But how did you know about me, Mother?'

'The Divine Mother told me,' she replied, 'I was to find and instruct three great beings striving for her blessings. I met two in the East. And today I have found you!'

Sri Ramakrishna fell at the Bhairavi's feet and said:

O Mother, I have so much to tell you. So much I need to know. What are these things happening to me? Haladhari says I'm insane. My body burns so I have to stand in water for hours to cool it. Am I going mad as they say? Can an intense yearning for God cause this?

The Bhairavi raised him up, smiled and said:

My son, this whole world is mad. Some are mad for wealth, some for pleasure, some for fame. Some for gold, for husbands, for wives or for little trifles. Mad for every foolish thing except God. And they understand only their own madness. When a man is mad after gold they have a fellow feeling for him, as lunatics think that only lunatics are sane. But if a man is mad after the Beloved, after the Lord, they think he has gone crazy. That is why they call you mad. But yours is the right kind of madness. Blessed is the man upon whom such madness descends.

The Brahmani took Sri Ramakrishna to Panchavati. She opened her bag of books and spread them: *Chaitanya Charitamrita* and *Chaitanya Bhagvata*. Quoting from the texts, the Brahmani told Sri Ramakrishna that when a powerful surge of divine emotions floods a human life, the gross body, unable to contain them, is often shattered by the stress. The burning pain in his body was a sign of an extremely rare state of *mahabhava*, the most exalted love of God, such as that experienced by the great Chaitanya and Radha of Vrindavan for Sri Krishna.

This pain, she said, could be relieved with sandalwood paste and flowers . . . For Sri Ramakrishna it was a revelation that texts, centuries old, should catalogue his experiences so precisely and matter-of-factly. It was a vindication beyond anything he might have imagined, that he was on the right path, an ancient and well-travelled way that eventually led him inevitably to a blessed union with God.

Once, Bhairavi Brahmani, as she came to be called in the context of her association with Ramakrishna, cooked some food as a part of her worship and offered it to the statue of Lord Rama. Closing her eyes she then went into samadhi. At that time Sri Ramakrishna, who wandered in the premises of Dakshineswar in a state of bliss, walked up to the statue, picked up the offering made by Brahmani and ate it with his eyes closed. Brahmani opened her eyes and watched without moving. At this juncture, Sri Ramakrishna came out of samadhi and realized what he had done.

He became completely distraught and said, 'Mother, why do I do these things? I don't know why I do these things. Here I am walking around asleep and I eat the offering you have made to Lord Rama.'

Bhairavi softly replied, 'My child, in eating this offering to Lord Rama, you have confirmed what was revealed to me in samadhi. Within you dwells an avatar of Ishwar who will soon be revealed to the world. You have only eaten what is your due.'

Sri Ramakrishna who was still feeling guilty was amazed by her reply and said, 'What are you saying, Mother!'

Bhairavi Brahmani picked up the idol of Lord Rama and worshipfully consigned it to the Ganga. The idol had fulfilled its purpose. The divinity that Bhairavi Brahmani, a nun of the Vaishnavite Shakti community of Jessore, had so tirelessly worshipped in stone had now appeared to her in the flesh.

Bhairavi was especially versed in tantric and yogic rites. From now on she brought all her spiritual powers to nurture the high intensity she glimpsed in Sri Ramakrishna. The attitude she spontaneously adopted towards her young charge was that of Mother Yasodha to her son Krishna in *vatsalya bhava*.

She guided Sri Ramakrishna methodically, meticulously and consciously – over past lives – by new routes to the same peaks of spiritual vision he had stumbled upon by the sheer intensity of his yearning. Central to tantra is learning to treat attraction and revulsion equally, with indifference. She took him through tantric sadhanas that revealed the divinity in ordinary objects and energies in the physical world, through the three modes of tantric worship – the animal, the heroic and the divine. And step by step through the awakening of the *kundalini*.

The term *kundalini* has been much used and much misunderstood. According to Hindu physiology, there is a great store of spiritual energy, the power of impulsion towards the godhead accumulated in past lives, coiled like a serpent at the base of the spine. This energy remains unmanifest in those who remain in bondage. When it is awakened, it leads man to a direct knowledge of the supreme consciousness that resides in the fontanelle at the top of the head, for this supreme consciousness always reaches out to the coiled power at the base of the spine.

Later, Sri Ramakrishna explained it succinctly, from his own experience.

> According to the tantric scriptures, the ultimate reality is *chit* (consciousness), which is identical to *sat* (being) and *ananda* (bliss). This ultimate reality or *satchitananda* is identical with the Vedic teachings. While man is identical to this reality, under the influence of maya or illusion, he has lost his true self. He has lost his identity between a world of subject and object and this error is solely responsible for his bondage and suffering. Therefore, the goal of spiritual discipline is the rediscovery of his true identity with the divine reality.

In order to achieve the goal of uniting the soul with the divine spirit, the Vedanta prescribes an austere method of discrimination and renunciation. This is very tough to follow, and, therefore, only a few individuals who are endowed with sharp intelligence and unshakeable will power can follow it to its very end. However, tantra does take into consideration the natural weakness of human beings – their lower appetites as well as their love for the concrete. It combines philosophy with rituals, meditation with ceremonies and renunciation with enjoyment. The underlying purpose of the entire process is to gradually train the aspirant to meditate on his identity with the divine spirit.

While the common man's aim is to enjoy the material objects of the world that come his way, the rules are different for those who resolve to tread a different and difficult path and to unite with the divine consciousness. Though tantra bids these individuals to enjoy the objects of the material world, it also preaches that they discover in every object, the presence of God. Mystical rites are performed and slowly the objects that they so desired earlier become spiritualized and this attraction is transformed into the love of God. Thus the very bonds of man are turned into treasures. The same poison that kills is transmuted into the elixir of life. Mere outward renunciation is not necessary because the ultimate aim of tantra is to sublimate *bhoga* or enjoyment into yoga or union with consciousness. According to this philosophy, the world with all its manifestations is nothing but the sport of Shiva and *shakti*, the absolute and its inscrutable power.

The discipline of tantra is graded to suit aspirants or students of all degrees. Exercises are prescribed for people with animal, heroic and divine outlooks. Certain rites require the presence of members of the opposite sex. Here, the student learns to look on woman as the embodiment of the Goddess Kali, the Mother of the universe. The very basis of tantra is the glorification of woman. Every part of a woman's body is to be regarded as a divine manifestation. But the rites are extremely dangerous and an aspirant must always seek the help of a qualified guru. An unworthy devotee may lose his foothold and fall into a pit of depravity.

According to the tantra system, *shakti* is the creative force in the universe. Shiva, the absolute, is more or less a passive principle. However, separating *shakti* and Shiva is as impossible as separating fire's power to burn from fire itself. *Shakti* contains the universe in its womb, and therefore, is considered to be the Divine Mother. All women are Her symbols and Kali is just one of Her several forms. Meditation on Kali is the central discipline of the tantra system. While meditating, the aspirant at first regards himself as one with the Absolute and then thinks that out of that impersonal consciousness emerge two entities, namely, his own self and the living form of the Goddess. He then projects the Goddess into the tangible image before him and worships it as the Divine Mother.

Sri Ramakrishna practised the disciplines of tantra and accepted Brahmani as his guru at the bidding of the Divine Mother. He performed profound and delicate ceremonies at Panchavati. He was often overwhelmed with a strange divine fervour and went into samadhi. In that state, evil ceased to exist and everything appeared as *lila* or the sport of Shiva and *shakti*. Every object that he beheld manifested the power and beauty of the Mother. The whole world, animate and inanimate, appeared to him as pervaded with *chit* and *ananda*.

Once, while he was in samadhi, he saw a vision of the ultimate cause of the universe in the form of a huge luminous triangle that kept giving birth, every moment, to an infinite number of worlds. He heard the animate *shabda*, the great sound Om, which echoes in the infinite sounds of the universe. He acquired the eight supernatural powers of yoga, which make a man omnipotent. But Sri Ramakrishna spurned these as valueless to the development of the spirit. He saw a vision of the divine maya, the inscrutable power of God, by which the universe is created and sustained and into which it is finally absorbed. He saw this form of maya in an exquisitely beautiful woman about to become a mother, who emerged from the Ganga and approached Panchavati slowly. Then she gave birth to a child and began to nurse it tenderly. A moment later she assumed a terrible form, seized the child by her jaws and crushed it. Swallowing it, she re-entered the water of the Ganga.

However, Sri Ramakrishna's most remarkable experience during this period of tantra sadhana was the awakening of the *kundalini shakti*, the serpent power. He actually saw the power, at first lying asleep at the base of the spinal column, then waking up and ascending along the mystic *Sushumna* canal and through its six centres, or lotuses to the *sahasrara*, the thousand-petalled lotus at the top of the head. He also noticed that as the *kundalini* went up, the different lotuses bloomed. This phenomenon was accompanied by different movements of the *kundalini* in the form of a fish, bird, monkey, etc. The awakening of the *kundalini* is considered to be the beginning of spiritual consciousness, and its union with Shiva in the *sahasrara* ending in samadhi, is the consummation of the tantric disciplines.

As long as the mind is attached to the world, immersed in passion, lust and greed, with no higher ambition to achieve something greater, or there is no vision, the *kundalini shakti* remains in the lower centres of the spine – those on the same plane as the rectum, the genitals and the navel. When the mind learns to dwell at the level of the heart, man experiences his first spiritual awakening and sees light and joy all around him. When the *kundalini* reaches the fifth centre – that is at the throat level, a man ceases to speak about anything but God. The sixth centre is situated at the forehead, between the eyebrows. And when the mind reaches this centre, the man gets a divine vision, though a trace of the ego remains. Finally, when the mind reaches the seventh centre, man goes into samadhi. He becomes a knower of Brahman, united with Brahman. What he experiences then cannot be described in mere words.

It becomes only too clear at which level most of us dwell . . . Many spiritual aspirants at high levels of their spiritual quest develop psychic powers. There are reportedly eight, including the power of healing, of materializing objects, of shedding light from one's body . . . The ability to create miracles has a magnetism that few can deny, and the ensuing vanity becomes an obstacle to enlightenment. Sri Ramakrishna, however, quickly learned the folly of using those powers developed as a result of his austerities.

Once, Sri Ramakrishna and Hriday were walking towards the Kali temple when Sri Ramakrishna told Hriday with wonder, 'I hear the sound of the Universe. Om!'

Hriday said that he should tell Bhairavi Brahmani about this. To which Sri Ramakrishna replied, 'She said it might happen. *Anahata dhvani* . . . I can hear the Universal Soul.'

After completing the tantric sadhana, Sri Ramakrishna followed Brahmani in the disciplines of Vaishnavism. The Vaishnavas are worshippers of Vishnu, the all-pervading, the Supreme God, who is also known as Hari and Narayana. Of Vishnu's various incarnations, the two with the largest number of followers are Rama and Krishna.

Vaishnavism is exclusively a religion of bhakti. Bhakti is intense love of God, attachment to Him alone; it is of the nature of bliss and bestows immortality and liberation upon the lover. God, according to Vaishnavism, cannot be realized through logic or reason; and without bhakti, all penances, austerities and titles are futile. Man cannot realize God by self-exertion alone. For the vision of God His grace is absolutely necessary and this grace is felt by the pure in heart. The mind is to be purified through bhakti. The pure mind then remains forever immersed in the ecstasy of God-vision. It is the cultivation of this divine love that is the chief concern of the Vaishnava religion.

In order to develop the devotee's love for God, Vaishnavism humanizes God. God is then regarded as the devotee's parent, master, friend, child, husband or even beloved, where each succeeding relationship represents an intensification of love. These *bhavas* or attitudes towards God are known as *shanta, dasya, sakhya, vatsalya* and *madhura*. The various characters in Hindu mythology, for example, the rishis of the Vedas, Hanuman, the cowherd boys of Vrindavan, Rama's mother Kausalya and Radhika who was Krishna's beloved, exhibited, respectively, the most perfect examples of these forms. In the ascending scale, God's glory is gradually forgotten and the devotee realizes more and more the intimacy of divine communion. Finally, the devotee regards himself as the mistress of his beloved, and no artificial barrier remains to separate him from his ideal. No social or moral obligation can bind his soaring spirit. He experiences perfect union with his Lord. Unlike the Vedantist who strives to transcend all varieties of the subject-object relationship, a Vaishnavite wishes to retain both his own individuality and the personality of God. To him, God is not an intangible absolute, but Purushottama, i.e. the Supreme Person.

As Sri Ramakrishna moved around the temple premises after his austere sadhanas, which were directed and supervised by Brahmani, his physical body began to look different and as he walked by, people made all kinds of remarks. For example, 'How beautiful the madman looks today,' or 'It's as though golden beams are coming out of him. How can that be?'

When Sri Ramakrishna overheard these comments, he said, 'Mother, they are charmed by my outer beauty. But do they see the beauty of You who dwell within? Take it away, Mother, this superficial gloss.'

While meditating, Sri Ramakrishna once saw a vision that he would have many disciples and some would be fair-skinned. When he told Mathur Babu about his vision, he did not even imagine what the coming years would have in store for them.

The Kali temple of Dakshineswar became a favourite resort of devotees and sadhus. Some of them were Paramahamsas,

Great Swans that swim freely and joyously upon the waves of the world without being in any way stained by them. Sri Ramakrishna described them as children, seeing everything filled with consciousness, irrespective of whether they were relatives or strangers, seeing Brahman in everything and everybody.

Dakshineswar was home to many seekers of God and one incident was memorably witnessed by Sri Ramakrishna and Hriday. A filthy sadhu in a *longoti*, covered in dust, hair matted, blissfully danced and sang about how beautiful the world was and about the creation of *Parabrahman* in all his glory.

While dancing, the sadhu saw a garbage pile of discarded leaf plates and sat down, blissfully happy to eat the leftovers. Just then a dog also came to eat from the same garbage and the sadhu put his arm around the dog and both ate the same food. Hriday was disgusted and Sri Ramakrishna was surprised. He told Hriday that he was not an ordinary lunatic. He was possessed of God. To him the waters in a ditch were the same as the waters of the Ganga.

Later, Sri Ramakrishna found the Vaishnava monk sitting under a tree with a book and a pot of water. He seemed to be reading something very thoughtfully. Sri Ramakrishna approached the monk and respectfully asked him to show him what he was reading so reverentially. To Sri Ramakrishna's surprise, the sadhu showed him page after page of the book with just 'Rama O Rama' written on each of them. The monk asked Sri Ramakrishna what was the use of reading a whole lot of books. God could be found in the origin of the four Vedas and the eighteen Puranas. And His name equalled Him. So he was satisfied with His name alone.

Around the year 1864, there came another wandering Vaishnava monk, Jatadhari, whose deity was Rama and who always carried along with him a metal image of Rama in his boyhood. Jatadhari showed tender affection towards the image, which resembled Kausalya's love for her divine son, Rama. He

went around with food in his hand, fed the image and often
scolded it and said: 'Bad boy! You disappeared again! You are
shameless. Now eat!' Jatadhari treated him like a mother treats
a spoilt child, sometimes cajoling, chiding and sometimes
requesting Ramlala to behave and sometimes holding firm. As a
result of lifelong spiritual practice, he had actually found the
presence of his idol in this icon. Ramlala was no longer merely
an image made of metal, but a living God to him. He devoted
himself to nursing, bathing and feeding Rama, played with Him
and even took Him for a walk. And he found that the image
responded to his love and tender care. It was evident that
Jatadhari shared a unique relationship with the image of
Ramlala.

The subtle mind acts eternally on the gross body and the
body on the mind. One person's body and mind act on another.
There is a relation between the body and mind of the whole
world. The spiritual moods of loving God create changes in both
mind and body.

At this stage, Brahmani guided Sri Ramakrishna, the ardent
God lover, through the five moods of loving God, at which she
was adept. The simplest devotional attitude is *shanta bhava* – the
dualistic attitude of the worshipper to the worshipped – of the
created to the creator. It is a love that does not resemble any
human relationship. Sri Ramakrishna worshipped Ma Kali in
shanta bhava. In enacting Hanuman, the devotee of Lord Rama,
Sri Ramakrishna experienced *dasya bhava*, the mood of the child
to his parent or a servant to his master. Bhairavi directed him
into experiencing *sakhya bhava*, the love of the friend – as the
love of the shepherds for Lord Krishna. Now with Jatadhari's
Ramlala, Sri Ramakrishna experienced *vatsalya bhava*, the love
of the parent for the child.

He observed Jatadhari's relationship with Ramlala with great
love and interest. Once, when Jatadhari was annoyed with
Ramlala he got up and walked off in a huff. Completely

absorbed, Sri Ramakrishna's attention was riveted on the image. He picked it up, set it on his lap, looked at it in adoration, admonished it and said: 'You are a naughty one! Now go and call him back and eat a little.' Then Sri Ramakrishna set the image back on the floor. Jatadhari returned after some time and said, 'Will you come to me now? All right. Don't come . . . don't come.'

It was then that Sri Ramakrishna requested Jatadhari, 'Father, help me realize Ramlala as you have realized him. I see you surrounded by the bliss of His loving presence. Teach me, Oh Jatadhari, the secret mantra.'

Jatadhari, very peeved, said, 'But see, He neglects me now as never before. He wants to be with you!' Turning to the image he said, 'You do whatever you feel like. You have no feelings. You're unkind; you left your parents and went into the forest. Your father died of a broken heart.' He then picked up the image and left. But now, Jatadhari's ritual of feeding Ramlala was unsuccessful. He turned away to ladle out the food from the pot. On turning back he found the image had vanished. He sighed, sat back in tears and stared at the place where the icon had been. A light emanated from the vacant spot. Jatadhari was overwhelmed. Just then Sri Ramakrishna entered. Jatadhari fell at his feet and spoke with deep emotion:

> Ramlala revealed Himself to me. He has told me that He will not leave you. It fills me with joy to see Him happy playing with you. I will leave Him here with you and go my way.

Some days later, Jatadhari requested Sri Ramakrishna to keep the image and bade him adieu with tearful eyes. He declared that Ramlala had fulfilled his innermost prayer and he now had no need of any form of formal worship. A few days later, Sri Ramakrishna was blessed by Ramlala with a vision of

Ramachandra, whereby he realized that the Rama of the Ramayana, the son of Dasaratha, pervaded the whole universe as spirit and consciousness. Sri Ramakrishna realized that He is its creator, sustainer and destroyer. He is the transcendental Brahman, without form or attribute or name.

Vedanta teaches that there is no reality other than Brahman. Name, form, as we know them in the physical world, are merely illusions that must be overcome before Brahman can be known. The ego says, 'I am' therefore 'I am other than Brahman'. 'I am' is physically expressed as 'I have a body'. And from the body idea spring two others, mutually exclusive: I am a man, I am a woman. If a devotee can convince himself as belonging to the other sex, he is on the way to overcoming sex distinction – he will know the distinction is not absolute.

Sri Ramakrishna now devoted himself to scaling the most inaccessible and dizzy heights of dualistic worship, namely, the complete union with Sri Krishna as the beloved of the heart. He regarded himself as one of the *gopis* of Vrindavan, longing for her divine beloved. In his pursuit of love he forgot all about food and drink. He wept bitterly day and night. The yearning turned into a mad frenzy; for the divine Krishna began to play the same old tricks with him that He had played with the *gopis*. He teased and taunted, occasionally revealed Himself, but always kept a distance. Sri Ramakrishna's anguish brought back the old physical symptoms; the burning sensation while blood oozed out of the pores of his body, loosened the joints and brought his physiological functions to a complete halt.

The Vaishnava scriptures advise devotees to propitiate Radha and obtain her grace in order to realize Sri Krishna. So, the tortured devotee now turned his prayer towards Radha. In order to obtain her grace, Sri Ramakrishna requested Mathur to get him a woman's dress and jewellery. Only then did Sri Ramakrishna begin his new sadhana. Mathur got him a Benarasi sari, a gauzy *dupatta*, a *gharara* and a *choli*. Sri Ramakrishna admired the clothes, dressed himself as a woman in the sari, gave a coy look, minced his steps and fanned himself with a *chamara*.

Much to the amusement of the people, Sri Ramakrishna behaved like a woman, combed the hair of other women, gathered flowers, wore anklets and went about like a wealthy matron joining the other women when he entered the temple. Mathur, who was on the side reserved for men, was not able to recognize Sri Ramakrishna. When he did he was astonished.

And finally in *madhura bhava*, Sri Ramakrishna, always literal, always exact, unmindful of the opinions of others or scandals ensuing, enacted the role of Radha the milkmaid, whose love for Sri Krishna is unparalleled conjugal love, the culmination of the *pancha bhavas*, the *bhava* that encompasses all others.

As Radha, Sri Ramakrishna beat his head on the ground, wept and said, 'I cannot realize Radha, I cannot realize the love that Radha felt for Sri Krishna. The pain, the pain is unbearable. Oh, the pain of passion unfulfilled!'

Bhairavi consoled him and said, 'My son, this is the pain of separation from Brahman, from the Godhead. Your passion is the passion for reunion. Be patient, you are meant for union.' And then, after six months of sadhana, it happened. Sri Krishna revealed himself and fulfilled the longings of Sri Ramakrishna's soul. He experienced the joy of union and the agony of his soul vanished in the glorious realization of his beloved. He had obliterated sex distinction in his body. He had attained *madhura bhava*.

Some may feel Sri Ramakrishna's search for *madhura bhava* was unbecoming for a man. However, a vedantin knows that through long habit all thoughts are converted into *samskaras*. Obliterating the distinction between bodies brings us closer to the one undivided Supreme. All five *bhavas,* or moods of love, are subtle and purified forms of those mundane relations by which human beings are bound to each other in their daily lives.

In practising *bhavas* they understand, *jivas* can find their way to the Divine.

One day Sri Ramakrishna was seated with eyes closed and a devotee sat opposite him with a copy of the Bhagavad Gita. Sri Ramakrishna opened his eyes and saw a light emerging from a particular spot. An image of Krishna appeared in the light. Filled with wonder and happiness, Sri Ramakrishna saw that the light passed from Krishna's toe to the Bhagavad Gita and towards himself. As the light held the image of Sri Krishna, the book and the devotee in a triangle, Sri Ramakrishna perceived that God, his devotees and the scriptures, although they appeared to be distinct entities, were actually one.

He was now at the end of this phase of his sadhanas, and unknown to himself, Sri Ramakrishna was ready for union and for teachings in *advaita* – non-duality that leads to union with the Absolute.

If Sri Ramakrishna was indeed the divine manifest in human form, why did he need to be put through the sadhanas to experience that final unity with God? At first Mathur was inclined to mistrust Brahmani Bhairavi who took up so much of Sri Ramakrishna's time and taught him delicate and questionable tantric practices. Mathur thought to himself: 'Can such a beautiful woman be as pure as she seems?'

One day, as Mathur walked by the Kali temple, he mocked Bhairavi who came out of the temple: 'Well, Bhairavi, where is your Bhairava?' Bhairavi stopped, looked steadily at Mathur and pointed to the image of Shiva in the Kali temple. Mathur, still unconvinced, said, 'Ah, but that Bhairava is only stone! It doesn't move.' Bhairavi drew herself up and majestically replied: 'Why should I have become a Bhairavi if I cannot move the immovable?' Ashamed, Mathur walked away.

Mathur was bemused by Sri Ramakrishna and saw in him flashes of divinity. But he did not even suggest anything further for that would have opened the way to the young man becoming even more irresponsible. Mathur was chagrined when Bhairavi Brahmani not only maintained loudly that Sri Ramakrishna was an avatar, a reincarnation of the Lord Vishnu – as were Sri Rama and Sri Krishna – but she was ready to defend it formally, in debate with the most learned pandits.

Mathur, in two minds after he experienced Sri Ramakrishna's different facets, doubtfully told Bhairavi: 'The scriptures say there are only ten incarnations. Nine have already come, one, Kalki, is yet to come.' To which Bhairavi replied with marked certainty: 'Why? The Bhagavata records twenty-four and leaves space for many more.'

Mathur was not truly convinced with Bhairavi's reply. At her suggestion, a conference of eminent scholars was arranged to debate the matter.

Two famous pandits of the era were invited – Vaishnavacharan, the leader of the Vaishnava society, and Gauri. Vaishnavacharan arrived first with a distinguished company of scholars and devotees. Like a proud mother, Brahmani proclaimed her view before the great scholar and supported it with quotations from the scriptures. As the pandits discussed the deep theological question, Sri Ramakrishna was completely indifferent to everything that went on around him. He sat in their midst like a child, immersed in his own thoughts. Sometimes he smiled or chewed spice from a pouch. He even nudged Vaishnavacharan once and said: 'Look here, sometimes I feel like this too.' Finally, Vaishnavacharan arose and declared himself in total agreement with Brahmani. He declared that Sri Ramakrishna had undoubtedly experienced *mahabhava* and that it was the certain sign of the rare manifestation of God in a man. The people assembled there, especially the officers of the temple garden, were dumbstruck. Very innocently Sri Ramakrishna told Mathur: 'Just fancy, he too says so! Well, I am glad to learn that after all it is not a disease.'

A few days later, Pandit Gauri arrived, another round of meetings was held and he, too, agreed with the views of Brahmani and Vaishnavacharan. To Sri Ramakrishna's remark that Vaishnavacharan had declared him to be an avatar, Gauri replied, 'Is that all he has said about you? Then he has said very little. I am fully convinced that you are that mine of spiritual power, only a small fraction of which descends to earth from time to time, in the form of an incarnation.'

'Ah!' said Sri Ramakrishna with a smile, 'you seem to have quite outbid Vaishnavacharan in this matter. What have you found in me that makes you entertain such an idea?'

Gauri replied, 'I feel it in my heart and I have the scriptures on my side. I am ready to prove it to anyone who wishes to challenge me.'

'Well,' Sri Ramakrishna said, 'it is you who says so, but believe me, I know nothing about it.'

Thus, the insane priest was, by verdict of the great scholars of the day, proclaimed a divine incarnation. His visions were not the result of an overheated brain; they had precedents in spiritual history. But how did the proclamation affect Sri Ramakrishna himself? He remained the simple child that he had been since the first day of his life. Years later when two of his disciples openly spoke of him as a divine incarnation and the matter was reported to him, he said with a touch of sarcasm, 'Do they think they will enhance my glory that way? One of them is a stage actor and the other a physician. What do they know about incarnation? Why, years ago, pandits like Gauri and Vaishnavacharan declared me to be an avatar. They were great scholars and knew what they said. But that did not make any change in my mind.'

Divinity was ascribed to many spiritual leaders of all eras by wise men who had no idea or knowledge about what these great souls endured to attain enlightenment. Even Jesus Christ was ascribed divinity after his crucifixion. This is both an irony and paradox of life.

Sri Ramakrishna was a learner all his life. He was often found quoting this proverb to his disciples: 'Friend, as long as I live I learn.' When the excitement created by Brahmani's declaration was over, he decided to set himself the task of practising spiritual disciplines according to the traditional methods laid down in the tantra and Vaishnava scriptures. He pursued his spiritual ideal according to the promptings of his guru and set foot on mystic, traditional highways. All those who believed that Sri Ramakrishna was a madman agreed to accept the fact that he was not what their limited minds could comprehend.

A saint or *jivan mukta* is human, he is driven to be reborn by his history of actions to complete the cycles of karma by a virtuous life, and thereby evolve closer to the Godhead. He is still influenced by illusion, of matter, of maya, the game of Mother Kali. An avatar, however, has no karma that drives him. He is reborn as an act of grace for the good of humanity lost in *adharma*. When he reaches maturity he realizes his goal in life – to attain the Godhead, re-establish virtue, and show others the way. Although an avatar must, as he is born in human form, struggle against the spiritual blindness and ignorance that besets us all, he is ultimately the master of maya. A saint has little power to liberate others, an avatar does this by a touch, a glance, a word. What was Sri Ramakrishna? Was he an avatar? Or merely a saint? It depends on the quality of your belief.

Indian sages have said that God has three hundred million faces, each a symbol of a divine attribute. So many that it is not possible to know them all in a thousand lifetimes. Sri Ramakrishna, the devoted lover of God, now knew many attributes of the divine. He was intimately acquainted with Hanuman, Radha, Sita, Krishna, Rama, Kali, Shiva . . .

Yet something obscure still drove him on, some sense that his realizations, while wondrous, were yet incomplete. What more? He could not say. Nor could Brahmani who watched over her charge with such pure *vatsalya* devotion.

One day, yet another incident occurred. A well-built, supremely confident, handsome, tall and almost naked man arrived in Dakshineswar carrying a shining brass pot. His name was Totapuri and he arrived at the temple garden towards the end of 1864. Perhaps he was born in Punjab, where he was the head of a monastery and claimed to be the leader of seven hundred sannyasis. Totapuri was an *advaitin*, a *naga* monk versed in the theory and practice of Vedanta or non-dualism. After forty years of strict sadhana, he had achieved *nirvikalpa* samadhi, the highest level of spiritual attainment, where all the varied and multiple forms of the universe merge into the Eternal, the Immensity without a name, the Absolute. He looked upon the world as an illusion. He regarded the gods and goddesses of dualistic worship to be mere fantasies of the deluded mind. According to him, prayers, ceremonies, rites and rituals had nothing to do with true religion and he was utterly indifferent to them. Exercising self-exertion and unshakeable will power, he had liberated himself from attachments of the senses. He had practised austere discipline on the banks of the sacred Narmada for four decades, and had finally realized his identity with the Absolute. Since then he roamed the world as an unfettered soul, a lion free from the cage. Clad in a loincloth, he spent his days under the canopy of the sky, in storm and sunshine, feeding his body on the slender pittance of alms. He visited the estuaries of the Ganga. On his return journey along the bank of the sacred river, he stopped at Dakshineswar, led by the inscrutable Divine Will.

Unlike Brahmani, Totapuri received no messages from God. He was not looking for anyone. Now, everything material seemed unreal to him. The world was empty of substance, the more he saw of it the less real its fleeting images became. His face was devoid of expression as if he was totally disinterested.

Sri Ramakrishna sang at the time when Totapuri arrived. Making his way through the people straight to Sri Ramakrishna,

Totapuri abruptly said, 'My son, I see in you a soul that has travelled already far along the path of truth. If you wish it, I will help you reach the next stage. I will teach you Vedanta.'

Sri Ramakrishna looked at him, stood up in delight and said, 'Vedanta? Oh yes . . . Ah, but I don't know. I will have to ask Mother. She knows all.'

Totapuri, not knowing which mother Sri Ramakrishna meant, replied in an amused way, 'Very well, ask her. I am not here for long.' Sri Ramakrishna walked straight towards the Kali temple, returned after a conversation with the Mother and said happily and naively, 'Mother said She has brought you here for the very purpose of teaching me non-dualism.'

Totapuri sternly told his newly acquired student that before he studied the truth of Vedanta, he would have to take sannyas. 'Are you prepared?'

Sri Ramakrishna readily agreed and said, 'I am. But I want to spare my old mother who will be very hurt if I become a wandering monk!' Amused, Totapuri replied, 'Then I will take you through the rituals in secrecy.'

Sitting around a small *dhuni* fire with Totapuri, Sri Ramakrishna's head was shaved off, a tuft of hair was thrown into the fire along with the sacred thread. Then Totapuri handed an ochre robe to Sri Ramakrishna. Wearing his new robe, Sri Ramakrishna sat in front of Totapuri ready to take initiation from his new master. He prostrated himself before him and took the oath of an aspiring sannyasi: 'I give up this moment the desire of attaining the bliss and other worlds. All beings of the universe will be free from fear on my account.'

Totapuri began his instructions:

Nirguna, Nirakara Brahman is the only reality. The one substance, ever pure, eternally awakened, ever free, unlimited by time, space and causation. Maya divides the One into names and forms, but Brahman is indivisible . . . Give up

this unreal world of maya. Break the iron cage of name and
form and leap out like a lion. The world of name and form
will vanish into nothing. Dive deep into the reality of your
atman, existing only in your innermost Self. Let your puny
ego merge into Cosmic Consciousness, where it will cease
to function. And you will know Satchitananda. You will
merge into Brahman in *nirvikalpa* samadhi.

He then recited certain vows and Sri Ramakrishna repeated
what he said:

> *I will merge into the Brahman.*
> *May the truth of the supreme Brahman reach me.*
> *May the truth of the supreme Brahman reach me.*
> *May the sweet bliss of the One, Undivided, Eternal,*
> *manifest itself in me.*
> *May the sweet bliss of the One, Undivided, Eternal,*
> *manifest itself in me.*
> *O Supreme Self who has the power to reveal Brahman*
> *consciousness in all his children, may I your child and*
> *servant be an object of special compassion.*
> *O Supreme Self, who has the power to reveal Brahman*
> *consciousness in all his children, may I your child and*
> *servant be an object of special compassion.*

Totapuri continued, 'Get rid of those intruding webs of maya
– dive deep into the atman, into Paramatman. Get rid of all
thoughts by steeling your mind. Say "not this'', and as another
thought comes up, say "not this . . . *neti, neti* . . . Brahman is not
this".'

Once, when Sri Ramakrishna was in deep meditation he saw a light that emanated in the space ahead. The objects in the hut merged into Ma Kali. Totapuri entered, examined his student and frowned. Sri Ramakrishna opened his eyes and said, 'I see the Mother. Always, I see the forms of the Mother. No, no. I cannot stop my Mind and dive into the Self beyond.'

Totapuri got very excited and said, 'Why not? Why not? It *must* be done!'

Sri Ramakrishna pleaded with him, 'I cannot make my mind free from matter. I must see the many glories of the Mother.'

Totapuri replied fiercely, 'No! I say you must get past her. She is maya. It must be done!'

Totapuri looked around and found a piece of broken glass, picked it up, pierced the point between Sri Ramakrishna's eyebrows with it and said, 'Collect the mind here – at this point.' Once again, Sri Ramakrishna closed his eyes and saw light emanating in the space ahead. He saw Ma Kali's image as it dissolved in an oval nimbus of light.

Almost wailing now, Sri Ramakrishna spoke, 'Even from this form must I free my mind?' And answered his own question with determination, 'Yes, Yes, this too I must do.' But the form remained and he whispered, almost afraid, '*Neti, neti* . . . not this . . . Let my knowledge be a sword . . . not this.' Then he saw that a glass sword cut the luminous image of the Goddess in two. There was a swirl of colour and form which disappeared into waves.

Totapuri examined Sri Ramakrishna carefully and slowly got up. Leaving him in that state of being, he settled himself for meditation under a tree. Hriday came to him and said, 'Forgive the intrusion, Master, but Sri Ramakrishna has not eaten for three days.'

Totapuri replied, 'No, no. Do not disturb him. I will see to him myself.' He entered the hut and found Sri Ramakrishna in the same position with a calm and serene face. He put a finger under Sri Ramakrishna's nose and his hand on his throat. Then he pushed Sri Ramakrishna, who had become like a stone. Totapuri was joyous and could not believe what had happened and said in amazement, 'This is a miracle! It took me forty years of austere sadhana to accomplish this. He has done it in three days! This is indeed *nirvikalpa* samadhi, a Divine Miracle.'

Some years earlier, Sri Ramakrishna's impulse to end his own life by the ceremonial sword of Kali had effectively rent the veil of normalcy and the incomparable form of Kali in *savikalpa* samadhi, the highest ecstasy in the realm of form, had flooded his consciousness. For a moment he had gone beyond form to experience the formless ocean of consciousness, Brahman without beginning or end that filled the universe with compassion and love. But he had been unable to remain united with the ultimate – the personal form of Brahman. Now, taking up the sword and slaying that which was dearest to him – the beloved image of Mother Kali, Sri Ramakrishna soared again beyond the known.

This time the break was more radical. In putting the Mother, on whom he so depended, to the sword, Sri Ramakrishna severed life's last tenuous thread to striving and desire. His senses and mind stopped functioning. Only the faint consciousness of 'I' repeated itself in rythmic monotony for a time, and soon even that ceased. What remained was existence alone. Sri Ramakrishna had in rapturous ecstasy become one with the Brahman. He gazed no longer at the face of the Absolute, but from it.

Totapuri was chanting 'Om . . . Om . . . Hari Om . . . Hari Om . . . Hari Om' when Sri Ramakrishna opened his eyes and smiled. Witnessing his students' progress, Totapuri's face beamed with joy. Sri Ramakrishna, after unlocking his joints, prostrated in front of Totapuri who picked him up, embraced him with tears in his eyes and admiringly said, 'I usually do not stay more than three days in any one place, but now I do not know when I shall leave.'

Totapuri was possessed of many good *samskaras*. He suffered from no vagaries of the mind; he believed in self-effort and self-reliance as determining factors in a man's life. His independent temperament inclined him towards spiritual discrimination rather than devotion. Logically, he was forced to accept the existence of Kali as the Mother of duality, of the variety of the universe and the source of the fruits of action – karma, but he did not feel the need to approach Her with love and submission. The idols of Kali and Krishna were to him just clay and metal. He was sure that Sri Ramakrishna would give up his superstitious, dualistic worship once he began to practise non-dualistic sadhana. But achieving *advaitic nirvikalpa* samadhi did not stop Sri Ramakrishna from continuing his *dvaitic* devotion to Kali and Krishna, Ram and Radha.

The ways of the Divine Mother seem to be strange. Sri Ramakrishna's so-called teachers, who helped him move from the realm of matter to that of spirit, taught the intricacies of their science to the best of their knowledge, but they too learnt some of their greatest lessons from their stellar pupil, which no austere spiritual training would have given them.

One evening, as Sri Ramakrishna was chanting and clapping his hands singing, 'Hari bol, Hari bol . . . Hari is Guru . . . Guru is Hari . . . the mind is Krishna, prana is Krishna, knowledge is Krishna, meditation is Krishna . . .,' Totapuri mocked him and said derisively, 'What? Are you making chappatis?' Sri Ramakrishna laughed and replied, 'Shame on you! You compare taking the name of God with making chappatis?'

Totapuri, who thought his student was swaying from his path, answered with a frown, 'You have been united with the Absolute, yet you continue to worship the Absolute as though he were the other. You seem to accept the world where people of lower evolution need images and attributes to worship! Do you forget that Brahman is the One and all others merely manifestations of maya. Maya can have no power over an enlightened soul.'

Sri Ramakrishna smiled and carried on. Just then a gardener approached the *dhuni* and began to light his hookah (a traditional smoking pipe). Irritated at the intrusion, Totapuri admonished him, 'What impertinence! Are you working for a temple or a rest house? How dare you defile the sacred fire?' He raised his hand to beat the servant with a pair of tongs. Seeing this, Sri Ramakrishna laughed. This surprised Totapuri who asked, 'What? You laugh at his insolence?'

Sri Ramakrishna's response was profound, 'Were you not just telling me that Brahman alone is real and everything in the universe is merely its manifestation? Yet the next moment you forget all and are ready to beat one of Brahman's manifestations. I laugh, Master, not at the servant's insolence, but on seeing the irresistible power of maya!'

Totapuri was stunned. Staring at his pupil he replied with humbleness, 'Yes, you are right. I forgot Brahman in my anger. Passion is indeed a dangerous enemy. I shall never give way to anger again.'

Sri Ramakrishna laughed gently and said, 'Good. But that is not the point I was making.'

Totapuri had no idea of the struggles of ordinary men in the toil of passion and desire. Having led an austere life throughout, he laughed at the idea of a man being led astray by his senses. He was convinced that the world was maya and man only had to fight maya and denounce it, for it to vanish forever. A born non-dualist, he had no faith in the concept of a personal God. He did not believe in the terrible aspect of Kali, much less in Her benign aspect. Music and the chanting of God's holy name made no sense to him. He ridiculed the spending of emotion on the worship of a personal God. He had a strong constitution and had little experience of the physical ills that beset most. He owned little, stayed nowhere longer than a few days. Eschewing material comforts he slept outdoors under the sky all round the year. His belief in the non-reality of maya made him scorn his body.

One day Sri Ramakrishna went to Totapuri, who was meditating, and sat quietly next to him. When Totapuri opened his eyes, Sri Ramakrishna asked, 'You have reached the ultimate . . . why must you meditate regularly, like a novice?' Totapuri picked up his shining brass pot and haughtily answered, 'Do you see how this sparkles? Suppose I were not to polish it every day? Would it not lose its lustre?' To which Sri Ramakrishna gently replied. 'Not if it were gold.'

It was time for the tables to turn. One day Totapuri suddenly clutched his stomach and seemed to be in pain. Sri Ramakrishna asked him with concern if he was unwell. Totapuri replied quite unconcernedly, 'Just stomach cramps. A strong mind rises above pain. Pain cannot be a deterrent – it is only an aspect of maya. Vedanta teaches us it is the mind that creates the body's ills. Great is the mastery of the mind over the body.'

Sri Ramakrishna smilingly said, 'Then why is your body out of control?'

Totapuri tried to smile with difficulty and said, 'It will pass. I do not remember experiencing pain before this.'

Totapuri clutched his stomach and lay down and Sri Ramakrishna hurried away to fetch Hriday and a *vaidya*. The *vaidya* squatted and felt Totapuri's pulse. Totapuri roughly protested and said he didn't need medication. Hriday then told him that he suffered from dysentery – owing to the climate. The pain was unbearable. Totapuri gritted his teeth and said, 'When I start losing that control, no physical pain will be able to bind me.'

The perplexed Hriday asked, 'I do not understand, Master?'

Totapuri very confidently stated, 'I will have no further use for this body.'

Sri Ramakrishna then told him, 'To discard your own body is to retard your spiritual development.' Totapuri explained that he had achieved *nirvikalpa*, so 'the purpose of my body is fulfilled. I may do with my body as I wish.'

The *vaidya* watched all this. He took Sri Ramakrishna aside and told him that Totapuri's condition looked very bad. 'He is remarkable. Anyone else would have howled like a hyena with all that pain.'

It was a moonlit night. Totapuri lay with a thin cloth covering him and groaned in pain. He finally got up and headed to the Ganga. 'Since I am not my body, I will associate with it no more. Better to end its pathetic existence in the Ganga. I've achieved *nirvikalpa*.'

Totapuri descended into the ghat, waded into the water and walked on, then looked at the water in astonishment and said, 'The water? What's happening? I'm always knee deep no matter how far into the river I go! How is this possible?' He looked around at the horizon. 'Where are the ships? Drowned in the sand? What a mysterious play of the Lord. I cannot even drown!'

Totapuri looked down and then up. At eye level he saw an effulgence in front of him. The effulgence spread and out of it came Mother Kali. The image spread over the water, the banks, trees and Totapuri saw himself transformed from pain to wonder. He began to sob like a child and said, 'Mother, Mother, Mother, Mother! Mother the Unthinkable Power! Mother is Land and Mother is Water. The body is Mother. The mind is Mother. Illness is Mother and health is Mother. Knowledge is Mother and ignorance is Mother. Everything I see and hear and imagine is Mother. She makes the nay and She makes the yea. O Mother Maya. As long as one is in the body one is not free from Her. Mother Kali, Shakti. How long have I deluded myself that I am the master of my destiny? Now you have shown me I am helpless in the face of the overwhelming forces of maya. I have thought the mind to be omnipotent. How wrong I have been. Shiva Shakti are One!'

After this experience, Totapuri waded back to the shore and returned to his sheet and brass pot. After that eventful night he was a calmer and a less haughty person. Then Sri Ramakrishna came up to him and said, 'You look well, Master.'

Totapuri related all that had happened and said, 'This disease has been a friend to me, Sri Ramakrishna. Last night I realized Brahman and maya are one. Brahman and *shakti* are one like fire and heat! To discriminate between the unseen power and the medium of its manifestation is self-deception. Ah, how ignorant I have been all these years. I thought my intellect, my will and good health made me a sovereign of all I surveyed. Now I know the Mother sent me here for two purposes: to teach you and to learn from you. Now I know why I have not been able to leave.'

Totapuri prostrated himself in front of the image of Kali inside the temple and prepared to leave. He embraced his pupil and left with a peaceful face.

Totapuri came for a few days but he stayed eleven months. He came with the hauteur of the *jnana* yogi, the blind spot of the intellectual. Born out of his knowledge of the One, the unity beneath the diversity of the universe, attained by will power and intellectual discrimination. He enabled his unexpected pupil to remain in the highest form of samadhi – Vedanta *advaitic* non-dualistic *nirvikalpa* samadhi, and left ennobled by his contact with a simple, uneducated temple priest, who taught him the necessity of devotion, and the humility to respect the multiple creations of the One.

Sri Ramakrishna, on the other hand, though fully aware like his guru, that the world was an illusory appearance, instead of slighting maya like an orthodox monist, acknowledged its power in the relative life. He was all love and reverence for maya, and perceived in it a mysterious and majestic expression of divinity. To him maya itself was God, for everything was God. It was one of the faces of Brahman – what he had realized on the heights of the transcendental plane, he also found here below and everywhere about him, under the mysterious garb of names and forms. And this garb was a perfectly transparent sheath, through which he recognized the glory of the divine immanence.

Maya, the mighty weaver of the garb, is none other than Kali, the Divine Mother. She is the primordial divine energy or *shakti*, and She can no more be distinguished from the supreme Brahman than the power of burning can be distinguished from fire. She projects the world and again withdraws from it. She spins it as a spider spins its web. She is the Mother of the universe, identical with the Brahman of Vedanta, and with the atman of yoga. She makes and unmakes laws; it is by Her imperious will that karma yields its fruit. She ensnares men with illusion and again releases them from bondage with a look of Her benign eyes. She is the supreme mistress of cosmic play and all objects – animate and inanimate – move by Her will. Even those who realize the Absolute in *nirvikalpa* samadhi are under Her jurisdiction, as long as they live on the relative plane of consciousness.

Thus, after attaining *nirvikalpa* samadhi, Sri Ramakrishna realized maya in an altogether new role. The binding aspect of Kali vanished from his vision. She no longer obscured his understanding. The world became the glorious manifestation of the Divine Mother. Maya became Brahman. The transcendental itself broke through the immanent. Sri Ramakrishna discovered that maya operated in the relative world in two ways, and he termed them *avidyamaya* and *vidyamaya*. *Avidyamaya* represents the dark forces of creation: sensuous desires, evil passions, greed, lust, cruelty. It sustains the world on the lower planes. It is responsible for man's cycle of birth and death. It must be fought and vanquished. But *vidyamaya* is the higher force of creation: the spiritual virtues, the enlightening qualities, kindness, purity, love, devotion, etc. *Vidyamaya* elevates man to the higher planes from *avidyamaya*; and he then becomes *mayatita*, that is, free of maya. The two aspects of maya are the two forces of creation, the two powers of Kali; and she stands beyond them both. She is like the sun, bringing into existence and shining through, standing behind the clouds of different colours and shapes and conjuring up wonderful forms in the blue autumn heaven.

The Divine Mother asked Sri Ramakrishna not to be lost in the featureless Absolute, but to remain in *bhavamukha*, that is, on the threshold of relative consciousness and tread the thin line between the Absolute and the relative. He was to keep himself at the 'sixth centre' of tantra, from which he could see, not only the glory of the seventh, but also the divine manifestations of the *kundalini* in the lower centres. He gently oscillated back and forth across this thin dividing line. Ecstatic devotion to the Divine Mother alternated with serene absorption in the ocean of absolute unity. He thus bridged the gulf between the personal and the impersonal, the immanent and the transcendent aspects of reality. This is a unique experience in the recorded spiritual history of the world.

Sri Ramakrishna, who embodies the highest aspiration of the path of devotion, went through the sadhanas, seeking an experience of non-duality under the tutelage of Totapuri. If Totapuri left Dakshineswar mellowed by the awareness that truth is not one- sided and is greater than any theory created by the intellect, Sri Ramakrishna's horizons had also broadened since his contact with the Absolute. The experience of *nirvikalpa* samadhi had stirred him more deeply than he could have imagined. Now he lived continuously in its shadow, as though some powerful undertow dragged him relentlessly towards the very centre of consciousness. And he was not inclined to resist.

Sri Ramakrishna resolved to drink deeply of the uninterrupted bliss of *nirvikalpa* samadhi. His already fragile interest in earthly life collapsed: food, sleep, ritual, love, hate, light, darkness, everything fell away for six timeless months. Ordinarily a yogi can remain in *nirvikalpa* samadhi for twenty-one days, after which the physical organism quietly falls away like an autumn leaf. And the *jiva*, the individual soul, dies never to be reborn, merged forever with the eternal in the vast ocean of consciousness.

Sri Ramakrishna remained in *nirvikalpa* samadhi without food or water. To the common man, who cannot distinguish between the spiritual and the profane, he looked like a dead man. After Haladhari, Akshay, a young, handsome, graceful boy of seventeen, was appointed priest of the Kali temple. He was Sri Ramakrishna's beloved nephew and was well-versed in scriptures since his childhood. Akshay was given the charge of looking after Sri Ramakrishna's needs.

Strangely, different people came into Sri Ramakrishna's life at different points of time to look after his physical and spiritual needs. They also left just as mysteriously as they came. Though some left their mortal coil, others just disappeared into thin air. Now it was Akshay's term to become custodian of Sri Ramakrishna's physical body. He was very worried and concerned about his uncle and ran from pillar to post seeking help from holy men who visited the Dakshineswar temple regularly. One day, Akshay went up to a sadhu visiting Dakshineswar at that time, and said, 'Maharaj, my uncle has been in samadhi for ten days and he has not eaten a morsel. He is not breathing . . . it is as if he is made of stone. The sadhu simply replied, 'I know,' rose and entered the hut where Sri Ramakrishna was meditating. Sri Ramakrishna was still in *nirvikalpa* samadhi and Bhairavi sat near him surrounded by religious texts. Hriday also stood there and Bhairavi said with concern to Hriday: 'I told him not to have anything to do with that naked fakir!'

Meanwhile, the sadhu went up to Sri Ramakrishna, felt his shoulder and prodded his fingers in his chest. Anxiously Akshay asked, 'Can you do something?' The sadhu nodded and said, 'I know the state.' He looked around, found a thin stick and beat him, gently at first and then more forcefully. Sri Ramakrishna took a long rattling breath while Hriday tried to stop the sadhu. He could not bear to see his uncle being beaten. But Brahmani held Hriday back so that the sadhu could achieve what he had

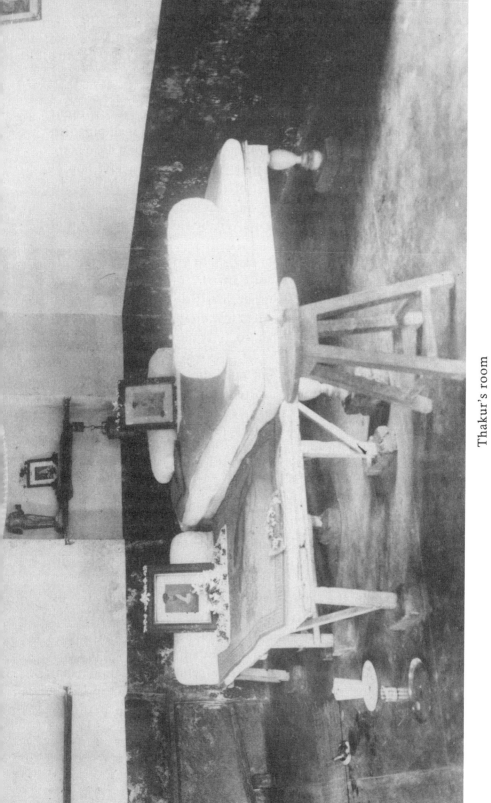

Thakur's room

set out to do. The sadhu then turned to Akshay and said, 'Arrange for some light, liquid food.'

Akshay hurried out and returned with a platter. The sadhu gently put a little of it into Sri Ramakrishna's mouth. Some of it got in and the body breathed painfully, the rest fell on his chest. Slowly the sadhu fed him, morsel by morsel.

It was a heroic struggle for six months. Whenever Sri Ramakrishna stirred even slightly into external awareness, the devoted sadhu thrust food and water down his mouth. At other times he beat his charge vigorously, till he had attained enough consciousness to be force-fed. Miraculously the tenuous flame of life flickered on. It was not until a severe bout of dysentery forced his attention back to his body, that Sri Ramakrishna re-entered the physical world again. Then the sadhu, who had providentially turned up and helped the Master regain his foothold, disappeared just as mysteriously without a trace.

Sri Ramakrishna was now gaunt and weak. Though he walked up and down, his face was impassive and the eyes far away. For him life and death had become equally unimportant. But for us it is crucial that he survived. Had he crossed the bridge, as no doubt he yearned to do at that time, he would have died leaving behind a faded memory of just another Indian holy man. There would have been no disciples, no flood of inspired teachings. One of the greatest legacies of the world's spiritual heritage would not have materialized. The living example that nourished and inspired Indians for a century and revealed the greatness of India's spiritual culture to the world would have evaporated without a trace.

Perhaps, he felt the needs of generations yet unborn, the needs of a world seemingly abandoned by God . . . and this forcibly drew him out of that radiant, nightless world, back into our uncertain world of shadows, darkness and light.

From this time on, Sri Ramakrishna began to seek the company of devotees and holy men. He had gone through the storm and stress of spiritual disciplines and mystic visions. Now, he realized an inner calmness and appeared to others as a normal person. But he could not bear the company of worldly people or listen to their talk. Fortunately, the holy atmosphere of Dakshineswar temple and Mathur's liberality attracted monks and holy men from all parts of the country.

Sadhus of all denominations – monists and dualists, Vaishnavas and Vedantists, *saktas* and worshippers of Rama – flocked there in ever-increasing numbers. Ascetics and visionaries came seeking Sri Ramakrishna's advice. Vaishnavas had come during the period of his Vaishnava sadhana, and tantrics when he practised the tantric disciplines. Vedantists began to arrive after the departure of Totapuri.

In Sri Ramakrishna's room, where he was recovering from dysentery, the Vedantists engaged in scriptural discussions. Forgetting his own physical suffering, Sri Ramakrishna solved their doubts by referring directly to his own experiences. Many of the visitors were genuine spiritual souls, the unseen pillars of Hinduism, and their spiritual lives were quickened in no small measure, by the sage of Dakshineswar.

Sri Ramakrishna, in turn, learnt from them the ways and conduct of holy men, which he subsequently narrated to his devotees and disciples. At his request, Mathur Babu provided him with large stores of foodstuff, clothes and other necessities for distribution among the wandering monks.

Though he had not read books, Sri Ramakrishna possessed an encyclopaedic knowledge of different religions and religious philosophies. This he had acquired by coming in contact with innumerable holy men and scholars. He also had a unique power of assimilation. With the help of meditation he made this knowledge a part of his being. Once, when a disciple asked him about the source of his seemingly inexhaustible knowledge, he replied, 'I have made a garland of their knowledge, wearing it round my neck, and I have given it as an offering at the feet of the Mother.'

Sri Ramakrishna would say that when the flower blooms, bees come to it for honey of their own accord. Many souls began to visit Dakshineswar to satisfy their spiritual hunger. He, the devotee and aspirant, became the Master. Gauri, the great scholar who was one of the first to proclaim Sri Ramakrishna an incarnation of God, paid the Master a visit in 1870 and with his blessings renounced the world. Narayan Shastri, another great pandit who had mastered the six systems of Hindu philosophy and had been offered the lucrative post of Court pandit by the Maharaja of Jaipur, met the master and recognized him to be the one who had realized those ideals in life, which he himself had encountered merely in books. Sri Ramakrishna initiated different people into different spiritual disciplines according to their needs and desires.

But this was not exactly what Sri Ramakrishna's heart was yearning for. His life was guided and guarded at every step by the Divine Mother. Sri Ramakrishna returned from his pinnacle of ecstatic knowledge to a world disinterested in what he had to reveal. Yearning to share his vision with those who might understand, his spiritual children, Sri Ramakrishna grew ever lonelier. But the great Mother had yet more sadhanas in store for him, before his disciples would arrive.

At Dakshineswar people of other faiths were welcomed. But till now, Sri Ramakrishna's attention had been absorbed by the images and attributes of the faith in which he was born. Govinda Rai, a Kshatriya, was a seeker of Truth. He had studied many religions and had finally become a Sufi. Sri Ramakrishna met Govinda Rai very warmly and asked him, 'My brother, what does Islam teach?' Govinda Rai replied that there is only one God. That He has created man and between men there is no high or low, only universal brotherhood. And Muhammad was the Prophet sent to tell us of the word of God.

Sri Ramakrishna, greatly interested, said, 'Tell me about the Prophet.' To which Govinda Rai replied, 'Allah sent prophets to interpret Him to man. There were many prophets before Muhammad – Moses and Jesus.'

Sri Ramakrishna responded like a child, 'Indeed! Avatars?' And Govinda Rai explained that Prophet Muhammad came at a time when man's mind had evolved so much that he was fully able to comprehend the divine reality.

Sri Ramakrishna, with childlike enthusiasm, pleaded, 'I also want to experience this divine reality . . . will you initiate me into the practice of Islam?'

Govinda Rai, momentarily astonished and speechless, replied, 'Yes I . . . I will be most happy to do so! There is a strict regimen – there is great emphasis on regular prayers.'

The God-loving if not God-mad Sri Ramakrishna needed no incentive to allow himself another form of sadhana and he eagerly said, 'Teach me all that, brother . . . teach me.'

Ready for this new form of sadhana, Ramakrishna dressed himself like a Muslim with a prayer cap and carried his rosary beads with him. The teacher, Govinda Rai, led the prayer and Sri Ramakrishna implicitly followed him: *Allah Ho Akbar! Allah Ho Akbar! Allah Ho Akbar! Allah Ho Akbar!*

This new practice was absolutely sacrilegious for the people at Dakshineswar. Hriday went to Akshay, who had silently watched the whole ritual and said, 'Are you following in your mad uncle's footsteps – going to Panchavati?'

Akshay, offended by this disrespect, replied, 'He's not mad – don't call him mad.' Hriday continued to be nasty and said, 'Then what is he doing "Allah Allah" all day and night?' Stung further, Akshay mocked, 'Why do you say "Ma Kali Ma Kali" all day and night?'

Hriday turned away, muttering in disgust, 'I should have known better than to say anything to you. But I'm warning you, he's leaving the temple – he's packing up to go to the mosque and live there.' And he left the place in disgust. Soon, the news of Sri Ramakrishna's new venture reached Mathur, who worriedly said, 'Here's another scandal! People are laughing again. But this time there's also anger. Why can't he just practise the sadhanas without making a display—wearing Muslim clothes! How difficult it is to protect your uncle! Now he tells me he wants to eat beef!'

Sri Ramakrishna observed the diet of the Muslims, sang *qawwalis*, grew a small beard on his chin, sat on a mat dressed like a Sufi saint and did his sadhana. The people around him watched helplessly and could do nothing to stop him, though it angered them immensely. After a few days of intense practice, Sri Ramakrishna saw a light in front of him and a man in a long robe and flowing beard appeared. Sri Ramakrishna seemed to recognize him and in a state of bliss said, 'Ya Muhammad! Ya Allah! Ya Muhammad! Ya Allah!'

In later years, Sri Ramakrishna spoke about this incident: 'I recited Islamic prayers five times a day, and felt disinclined to even see the forms of Hindu gods and goddesses, much less worship them. I spent three days in this mood. Then I experienced the form of Muhammad the Prophet, just as I had experienced Lord Rama and Sri Krishna. He merged into the formless Consciousness of Allah who is also Ishwar and Ma Kali.'

Well-intentioned liberals would like to believe there is no difference between religions and races. But there *is* a very big difference – on the surface, in the world of dualistic reality. Unity, as Sri Ramakrishna discovered through his own intimate experience, can only be found by going deep into the underlying non-duality of the all-projecting Universal Consciousness that manifests as Ishwar or Ma Kali, and also as Allah. Here, he experienced the dualistic vision of the Prophet merging into the non-dualistic one.

Sri Ramakrishna accepted the divinity of Buddha and pointed out the similarity between his teachings and those of the Upanishads. He also had great respect for the Tirthankara, who founded Jainism, and for the ten Gurus of Sikhism. But he did not speak of them as divine incarnations. He was heard saying that the Gurus of Sikhism were the reincarnations of King Janaka of ancient India. In his room at Dakshineswar he kept a small statue of Tirthankara Mahavira and a picture of Christ, before which incense was burnt every morning and evening.

Without being formally initiated into their doctrines, Sri Ramakrishna realized the ideals of religions other than Hinduism. He did not need to follow any doctrine. All barriers were removed by his overwhelming love of God. So he became a master who could speak with authority on the ideas and ideals of various religions of the world:

I have practised all religions – Hinduism, Islam, Christianity – and I have also followed the paths of the different Hindu sects. I have found that it is the same God towards whom all are directing their steps, although along different paths. You must try out all beliefs and traverse these different routes once. Whichever way I turn, I see men quarrelling in the name of religion. But they never reflect that He who is called Krishna is also called Shiva and bears the name of the optimal energy, Jesus, and Allah as well – the same Rama with a thousand names. A lake has several ghats. At one, the Hindus fill their pitchers with water and call it *jal*, but it is also called *pani* and water. The substance is one with different names, and everyone seeks the same substance; only climate, temperament and name create the minute differences. Let each man follow his own path. If he sincerely and ardently wishes to know God, peace be unto him! He will surely realize Him.

As clouds gathered over the Bengal skies, Mathur, fearful of the Master's health that always failed in the monsoons, dispatched him to Kamarpukur for the season.

In 1867, Sri Ramakrishna returned to his village to recuperate from the effect of his austerities. The peaceful countryside, the simple and artless companions of his boyhood, and the pure air did him a lot of good. The villagers were happy to get back their playful, frank, witty, kind-hearted and truthful Gadadhar, though they did not fail to notice the great change that had come over him during his years in Calcutta. His wife, Sarada Devi, now fourteen years old, soon arrived at Kamarpukur. Her spiritual development was far beyond her age and she was able to understand her husband's state of mind immediately. She became eager to learn about God from him and live with him as his attendant. The Master accepted her cheerfully both as his disciple and as his spiritual companion. Referring to the experiences of those few days, she once said, 'I used to feel always as if a pitcher full of bliss was placed in my heart. The joy was indescribable.'

Sri Ramakrishna was very warmly received in his village. As he and Hriday got off the bullock cart a man greeted him affectionately saying, 'Oh Gadai! Gadadhar! So you still remember us.' Then a little boy ran up to Sri Ramakrishna, embraced him and ran back in excitement announcing, 'Rameshwar da, Gadadhar da has come!'

The women of the village whose ears were full with gossip from Dakshineswar about Sri Ramakrishna's bizarre behaviour, talked among themselves: 'Is he as mad as they say? Let's go and see what he looks like.'

After alighting from the cart, Sri Ramakrishna, Bhairavi Brahmani and Hriday walked towards Sri Ramakrishna's childhood caretaker Dhani's home. Dhani the old maid, sitting in a veranda, still had a charming smile despite losing most of her teeth. Sri Ramakrishna and Hriday walked up to Dhani and greeted her. Unable to recognize them, Dhani asked who they were. Sri Ramakrishna said, 'Dhani Ma, you will know who in a minute. Bring out all the sweets in the house.' And indeed she

Holy Mother

knew him and said, 'Oh. It is Gadai!' And Sri Ramakrishna teasingly replied, 'What a way to greet me!'

Dhani, who was also a victim of all the gossip, said, 'Come nearer Gadai . . . let me look at you properly.' She felt his arms and face and said, 'You look quite sane to me.' Sri Ramakrishna promptly and affectionately responded, 'How can anyone brought up by you be sane?' Dhani, still stroking his arms, asked, 'Is it true that you dress as a woman and go around crying "Hari Hari"?' Sri Ramakrishna gave an affirmative reply and Dhani continued with her queries, 'Is it true that you say Musalmani beads and chant "Allah"?'

'Yes,' was the reply. Dhani gasped and looked at him shocked while Bhairavi Brahmani asked with annoyance. 'Do you jump around on trees like a monkey?' When Sri Ramakrishna said yes, yet again, Dhani was most puzzled. So Sri Ramakrishna asked, 'Hindu or Muslim, man or woman, monkey or human being . . . isn't it the same Brahman everywhere? As many faiths, as many paths . . . What is there so shocking about it, Dhani Ma?'

Dhani was astonished; she stared at him and said, 'You always did exactly what you wanted, Gadai.' And Sri Ramakrishna replied, 'All right . . . I am going to sing loud enough to bring Shiva himself down from Mount Kailash!'

Slowly, the courtyard filled up with village folk and people who came to see Sri Ramakrishna about whom they had heard the most absurd stories. As they watched, they changed their attitude, and their expressions of disapproval and vexation slowly became those of peace and adoration. Sri Ramakrishna settled down in the house of Rameshwar, his old family home, while they all celebrated his homecoming. During a conversation, Rameshwar asked, 'How is Akshay shaping?' Immediately Sri Ramakrishna assured him that he was a very devoted priest. 'After all, we are of the same blood aren't we?'

Rameshwar then enquired, 'And Mother? Is she well?' Sri

Ramakrishna answered that Mother would not leave the ghat of the Ganga anymore. 'I could not force her.' Hriday, looking appreciatively at Ramakrishna, interrupted, 'One thing you have to acknowledge, he is a worthy son. He spends time with her every day – every day when he is normal, that is . . .'

Brahmani, whose anger brewed by the minute compounded with a frustration that people were unable to see what she could, said it was not for ordinary people to judge the mental states of avatars. 'Leave it to them to talk about themselves.'

Every moment, every event and every happening seemed to be planned by the Divine Mother. All that happened in Sri Ramakrishna's life had a larger significance and one such event was to take place again. Saradamani, his wife, arrived with two male escorts, unannounced. Rameshwar's wife greeted her with joy and surprise and said, 'Oh Gadai, it's Saradamani. Come and see your wife, Gadadhar.' Sri Ramakrishna eagerly came out of the hut, followed by Rameshwar, to see Saradamani who bent and touched his feet. He helped her up and said, 'My wife! How she has grown! Give them all water! Give them something to eat!'

There was a lot of excitement in the house as each one went about in their efforts to make the guests comfortable. Sri Ramakrishna escorted Saradamani into the house and looked at her tenderly as at a child. Slowly, Saradamani got to know her new home and helped Rameshwar's wife with the household chores. One day Sri Ramakrishna called her while she was in the midst of some work and said, 'It is well that you help with the household chores, but your first duty will always be to God.' Saradamani meekly replied, 'I never miss my puja.' Indulgently but seriously, Sri Ramakrishna told her, 'That is good, but God must be forever in your heart. The image is only a means. Brahmani is my guru, so you must respect her as your mother-in-law. When I am not here, Prasanna, Dharamadas Laha's daughter, will guide you.'

Sri Ramakrishna instructed his young wife meticulously. While holding on to the ideal of detachment from the world on the one hand, he trained her carefully in the arts of household management on the other. Hours of inspired outpourings on God and devotion alternated with earthly instructions on how to shop for vegetables, trim a lamp, sweep the floor, receive guests. The madman of God now revealed a surprising peasant's shrewdness and practicality that was to be the underlying strain, as the seeker of God began his metamorphosis into the teacher of men. The natural pathway of Sarada's spirit, he saw, led not through restless strivings and passionate ecstasies, but through a quiet, purposeful dutifulness and attention to detail.

Taught and lectured by Sri Ramakrishna, Saradamani on one occasion fell asleep during a discourse. Prasanna was also there and tried to wake her up. Sri Ramakrishna gently told her, 'No, Prasanna, don't wake her.' Prasanna replied that she would be missing such priceless words. To which Sri Ramakrishna said, 'No, no. If she listens to everything I say, she will not stay on earth. She will unfold her wings and fly away.'

All along Bhairavi Brahmani watched Sri Ramakrishna and his wife Saradamani. She was not able to digest the idea of their mutual bonding, which grew stronger by the day. One day while Saradamani gave Sri Ramakrishna a glass of water, Bhairavi entered and burst out with the anger she had held within her for so many days. Speaking directly to Sri Ramakrishna, she said, 'I do not approve of your seeing so much of Sarada.' Sri Ramakrishna, surprised at this outburst, replied, 'I'm grooming her into spirituality, Mother. She is such a young girl.' And Bhairavi said, 'That is my worry. She is not only young but also pretty.' Sri Ramakrishna tried to reason with Bhairavi, 'Mother, you put me through so many tantric sadhanas with you. It is you who taught me to treat both attraction and repulsion in the same way.'

But Bhairavi wasn't appeased. She retorted, 'That was another matter. That was me. This is she. I have said what I had to say.'

Sri Ramakrishna, in a conciliatory way, told her, 'Totapuri used to say, "He alone is firmly established in the knowledge of Brahman who can keep intact his renunciation and discrimination even while living with his wife".' The further infuriated Bhairavi responded, 'Totapuri! All he can offer is dry knowledge.' Saradamani, who watched all this, was chased away by the angry Brahmani.

Whether due to jealousy or protectiveness Brahmani disliked anyone who was close to Sri Ramakrishna. For although she was such an evolved spirit, she was a *dvaitin*, a dualist, unable to understand or trust *advaita*. She detested Totapuri and instinctively disliked Saradamani. Every day, slowly, the stage was set for the final denouement, but when it came it was a fracas too minor to recount.

As we have observed, every stage of Sri Ramakrishna's life had significance, every act led to another turn in the drama of his life, which the Divine Mother had so carefully directed. One day, a person called Srinivas came for lunch. After the meal he said, 'Aah! I always eat so much at your house, Rameshwar da,' and reached out to pick up the leaf that served as a plate. Immediately Bhairavi said, 'Stop. Leave it. We do the cleaning ourselves.' Srinivas, surprised and embarrassed, left the leaf where it was and proceeded to wash his hands. Then a woman from the neighbourhood said sharply, 'He is not a Brahmin, we cannot clean up after him!' Bhairavi, equally stubborn, replied: 'But in his devotion to God he is higher than many Brahmins.' The neighbour insisted that it was the custom in their village. Bhairavi still angry, argued, 'Don't tell me your customs! Is devotion to be counted for nothing? Is love of the Divine not to be treated with respect?' The fight got steadily more serious with Hriday also joining in. Rameshwar's wife, who was distressed by this, tried to stop the quarrel. But Bhairavi was adamant, 'I am going to clean his plate right now.' Amidst all this noise Sri Ramakrishna pleaded with Hriday and Bhairavi not to quarrel. Hriday told Bhairavi authoritatively, 'If you do, we will not allow you to remain inside the house.' This shocked everybody, Rameshwar was stunned, and Bhairavi Brahmani, offended and outraged, left the house and walked away.

Saradamani and Rameshwar's wife begged Bhairavi not to leave. Unheeding, she went and sat under a banyan tree to meditate. Meanwhile, Saradamani anxiously asked Sri Ramakrishna whether she would come back. Sri Ramakrishna who knew Hriday had made a grave mistake said he did not know and added, 'Here everyone is always right! But she is my Guruma. She can do anything and we must give her love and respect.' Again Sarada asked, 'But she will come back, won't she?' Sri Ramakrishna just looked at her tenderly, acknowledging the anxiety and concern she felt on Bhairavi's departure.

Before she left, Bhairavi returned to put sandal paste, flowers and vermilion on Sri Ramakrishna. Prostrating at his feet, she said, 'Forgive me. I have erred in staying too long. A sannyasin and water must forever move on. That is the only way to keep pure.' Then Bhairavi picked up her things and left without looking back.

Sarada, unable to contain herself, ran after her, fell at her feet and asked Bhairavi to bless her. Moved by this gesture, Bhairavi said, 'Bless you my child, bless you.'

Sri Ramakrishna's journey through human sadhana had surfed through both the *dvaita* and the *advaita* – the dual and the non-dual. In Bengal to this day, the festival of Durga stirs every soul deeply. A vast cottage industry flourishes months before the festival, as clay images of Goddess Durga are made in the hundreds of thousands. To be worshipped with deep devotion for five days – only to be immersed thereafter in the Ganga, the nearest lake or stream. The reason for this ritual is not as mysterious as it seems; it is an exercise in understanding the essential source of divinity, the transience of material form.

Before the image of Durga is worshipped, the worshipper must transfer the divine presence from within his or her own heart into the image. After five days of prayer, the divine presence must be withdrawn from the image and reinstalled in the worshipper's heart.

Once, during Durga Puja, Sri Ramakrishna visited Mathur's house where the deity was being worshipped. After the scheduled puja days the deity was picked up with all due formality and ceremoniously offered to the Ganga. At this point, Mathur grabbed the arms of the carriers, tried to stop them and cried out in grief, 'No! No! She is the Goddess. You cannot drown the Mother!'

The attendants resisted but Mathur became violent. So they left the image and went to call Sri Ramakrishna as even Mathur's wife, Jagadamba, was unable to resolve the crisis. In Mathur's heart the image and the divine presence had merged. He threatened everyone against removing the image and became bloodthirsty. His household members feared that he too had become like his protégé, Sri Ramakrishna, and gone quite mad.

Meanwhile, one of the attendants returned with Sri Ramakrishna, who went up to Mathur and put his hand on his shoulder. Mathur still in a manic phase began to calm down when he saw Sri Ramakrishna. Rubbing Mathur's chest he said, 'What are you afraid of? Do you really think the Mother will leave you just because her image is immersed in the Ganga? Can a mother ever leave her child? She is within your heart.'

'Master, enlighten me with your touch,' Mathur had often begged Sri Ramakrishna. 'Show me what you see. I want to experience your ecstasy.' To which Sri Ramakrishna always replied, 'This ecstasy is not to be taken lightly, Mathur Babu. Be patient, keep your life balanced between devotion and worldly obligations for that is your dharma.' But Mathur always persisted. Eventually, Sri Ramakrishna said he would ask the Mother her opinion in the matter. Now with his touch, Mathur could experience the ecstasy he had longed for.

However, some days later, Mathur urgently sent for Sri Ramakrishna. When he arrived, Mathur staggered up to him, with flushed eyes red from weeping, feverishly fell at his feet and said, 'Baba, I am beaten. I have been in deep concentration for three days! I cannot think of my business however hard I try. Everything is going wrong.' Sri Ramakrishna gently and teasingly replied, 'But you begged me for ecstasy.' And Mathur pleaded, 'I know I did. But please, take back this ecstasy of yours; it suits only you. I didn't realize I would be so possessed by this . . . spirit that I would have to take every step and do everything just as it told me, twenty-fours hours a day.' Sri Ramakrishna rubbed Mathur's chest with his hand. As Mathur began to recover he smiled and said, 'Now I begin to feel my normal self again.'

The relationship of the worldly Mathur and the saintly Sri Ramakrishna was made up of strange alternations. At times, Mathur treated Sri Ramakrishna, many years his junior, like a revered spiritual father; at others, like an irresponsible boy. But Mathur, wealthy almost beyond count, always gave generously to Sri Ramakrishna, anything his heart could want. This was usually nothing, since money made no sense to him. But there were times when Sri Ramakrishna tried Mathur's generosity to the limits.

On 27 January 1868, Mathur, his wife Jagadamba, Hriday and Sri Ramakrishna set out from Howrah station in Calcutta, on a pilgrimage to some revered holy sites. The ever-ebullient Mathur organized the sojourn in royal style, reserving several coaches on the train for his party and attendants.

The first stop was at the Shiva temple at Deogarh. Here Sri Ramakrishna, overcome by the poverty of the villagers, demanded of Mathur: 'Give each person a piece of cloth, one meal and oil for their heads. After all,' he said, 'you're the keeper of Mother's estates.'

He overruled Mathur's appalled protestations about the cost of the journey, and that one man could not feed and clothe so many. 'These people have no one to look after them,' Sri Ramakrishna cried like a child. 'If you don't help them, even this little bit, I will not go with you to this Benares of yours, I will stay here and look after them.' Mathur acquiesced perforce, and sent for vast supplies from Calcutta.

In making this pilgrimage, Sri Ramakrishna traversed two distinct landscapes: the literal geography of temples, villages, forests, plains, wheat and rice fields . . . the landscape of the senses and the parallel, glorious dreamscape of the mind, of legend, myth and metaphor. The gap between the two can be confusing and painful; nowhere more so than in Benares where self-renouncing yogis and searchers of the spirit can be found along with hordes of pompous pilgrims, scheming priests, avaricious merchants, rumour and gossip.

At Mathurnath's Benares home, while listening to an endless conversation on profit and loss, Sri Ramakrishna cried out in anguish: 'Where have you brought me, Mother. I was better off in Dakshineswar.'

Then one day, he experienced the subtle essence of the city below its surface, bathed in a golden radiance of the spirit.

While at Benares, Sri Ramakrishna went to meet Trailanga Swami, the celebrated monk whom he later declared to be a real Paramahamsa, a veritable image of Shiva. Mathur told Sri Ramakrishna that Trailanga Swami never spoke, to which Sri Ramakrishna said, 'The truth is not found by these hypnotic words. The truth is found in silence.' Mathur also told Sri Ramakrishna about the incident when the British government had locked him up several times for roaming around naked in Benares. Hriday added, 'They think it is civilized to wear pants and coats even in the heat!' Sri Ramakrishna completing the story, said, 'I heard he was found asleep on the roof each time and the door was still locked.'

On reaching there, they found the three-hundred-pound, naked, bearded *muni* lying comfortably in the blazing midday sun. Seeing his size, Mathur said, 'How can the British possibly understand that, Baba!' Sri Ramakrishna fell at Trailanga Swami's feet and asked, 'Muni, I have a question to ask of you. Will you favour me with a response? Be it without words.' Trailanga Swami only nodded and the question was the eternal one to which there seem few answers: He asked, 'Is God one or many?' The muni made gestures with his hands, which Sri Ramakrishna interpreted and explained on his behalf. 'When man is in samadhi, he knows Brahman is one; when man is in normal consciousness aware of "I" and "you", Brahman is many.' He paused, turned to Hriday and continued, 'In Trailanga muni, Hriday, you see a true knower of Brahman.'

The pilgrims moved on to Allahabad where the party bathed in the holy confluence of the Ganga, Jamuna and Saraswati rivers, and then arrived at Vrindavan, where Lord Krishna lived as a child. Here, Sri Ramakrishna was in a state of continuous ecstatic excitement. He observed the cowherds, birds and gardens. 'Where is Krishna,' he cried, 'why can I not see him? Everything here is blessed by his presence. But where is *He*?'

It was here that he met the holy Ganga Mai, a devotee of Radha, reputed to be the reincarnation of one of Radha's handmaidens. Ganga Mai recognized in Sri Ramakrishna a reincarnation of Radha herself! And the two became as intimate as two friends at school. Sri Ramakrishna declared he would live the rest of his life in Vrindavan with his new friend . . . till he remembered his old mother living alone in the music tower, in Dakshineswar.

In the fifteenth century, Bengal had produced another God-mad saint, Sri Chaitanya. Much like Sri Ramakrishna, he also danced gleefully, in sudden spontaneity, to the heat of *mahabhava* coursing through him. His body needed to be cooled with sandal paste to facilitate his insights and visions. Sri Chaitanya was the founder of a Vaishnavite sect that believed he was an avatar of Lord Vishnu and that even after death, after attaining *mahasamadhi*, he would occupy his earthly seat in his subtle body. He was most revered, most holy.

In Vrindavan, a big hall had been built around the seat of Chaitanya where devotees sat and sang devotional songs. When Sri Ramakrishna entered the hall he went into samadhi. Suddenly he moved forward through the devotees and jumped on to Chaitanya's seat with his hands raised saying, 'Hari bol, Hari bol.' For a moment the devotees were shocked, but soon joined him chanting 'Hari bol'. Some devotees praised him, 'Here is the incarnation of Sri Chaitanya. Victory to the Divine Lord.' While others criticized, 'This is sacrilegious. We must report this. How can any man, however saintly, presume to dance on Sri Chaitanya's seat? We did invite him. But not to desecrate the seat of Lord Vishnu's avatar.'

Meanwhile, the devotees reported this bizarre behaviour to the resident priest, Babaji Bhagawan Das, who scolded some devotees at the time, 'If you carry on this way, I will personally confiscate your beads.' Suddenly, Babaji felt that he was unable to continue and said, 'It seems to me some great soul is nearby.' By then the message about a mad man sitting on Sri Chaitanya's seat reached him and he said, 'I don't know what this world is coming to – some mad man dances on Sri Chaitanya's seat and all you buffoons do nothing about it!' Turning to a devotee he admonished, 'I will throw you out of the Vaishnavite community, you fool.' Just then Hriday went up to Babaji and said, 'Babaji, my uncle loses himself in the name of God and has been doing so for a long time now. He has come to visit you.' Babaji looked at him eagerly and asked, 'Yes? I had the feeling . . . Tell me about him? Where do you come from?'

Just then Sri Ramakrishna shyly entered the doorway, swathed from head to foot in a white sheet and quietly sat at the back. Hriday with naive curiosity continued, 'Babaji, why do you use beads? You have attained enlightenment; you no longer need them.' He replied absentmindedly, 'This is true I don't need them. But since my disciples always do what I do, I must set an example or else they will go astray.'

Sri Ramakrishna who sat silently in the audience had enough of all this and got up saying, inspirationally and impersonally, 'How is it you are so egotistic even now? Is that how you think of yourself? You think you'll teach the people? That you'll expel them from your community? You think you can decide when you'll give up telling your beads? Who made you a teacher? Do you think you can teach the world unless the Lord who made it allows you?'

At first Babaji frowned and Mathur got worried, but gradually a clear understanding dawned and he answered humbly, 'No one has spoken to me this way for many years; I am surrounded by sycophants. You are right, Master; I have lost my way. I knew a great soul was nearby, and I was right.' Delighted, Babaji fell at Sri Ramakrishna's feet. 'I am honoured, Master, that you should come to see me . . . Now I see you are the incarnation of Sri Chaitanya.' Sri Ramakrishna raised him by his shoulders and embraced him.

From 1868 to 1871, Sri Ramakrishna travelled incessantly, learning about the spiritual and physical conditions of the people, about their religious ideas and visiting holy places. Those with spiritual powers visit sacred places not to take, but to replenish them with the same spiritual powers that the masses draw daily from them.

In this period, he not only visited the holy places of the Hindus in Calcutta and its surrounding areas, but also those of the Christians such as the Holy Trinity Church on Ram Mohan Sarani, and the Methodist Church on Surendra Bannerjee Road;

and those of the Muslims such as the Garatollah Masjid on Chittaranjan Avenue in Calcutta and the Mallapura Masjid near Dakshineswar. The Eden Gardens, Fort William, the Asiatic Society Museum and the Alipore Zoo were not off his itinerary – life did not exist only in the realms of the spirit!

Death is the inevitable end of our physical lives, our final destination, and our unavoidable final truth. Yet we deny it for we are knitted into our bodies, entwined in our relations with our kin; we suffer grief and loss; given the choice we would live, if we could, forever, bound inextricably into our material manifestations close to our families and friends.

Of all his relatives, Akshay was the closest to Sri Ramakrishna. The son of his eldest brother Ramkumar, the priest of the Kali temple after Haladhari, a young man of a charming, open, sunny disposition. However, Akshay became terminally ill. He was looked after by Mathur, his grandmother Chandra Devi and Sri Ramakrishna himself. At his deathbed, Ramakrishna recalled all that happened while Akshay was around. The way he dressed Akshay as the child Krishna, the way he used to chant prayers in Kamarpukur and the way he and an unknown sadhu looked after Sri Ramakrishna in his *nirvikalpa* samadhi. This was another mysterious plan of the Divine Mother. Akshay was needed at a particular time in Sri Ramakrishna's life and now that need was no longer there. His future needs involved other people who were all ready or would soon be designated.

As Sri Ramakrishna and Chandra Devi sat by Akshay's deathbed, Chandra Devi sorrowfully said, 'He only just got married.' Sri Ramakrishna added, 'Send for a doctor. What else can we do?' He paused, then said, 'He will die anyway.' These words shocked everybody and Sri Ramakrishna himself realized what he had said and shook his head. As he watched his beloved nephew die, Sri Ramakrishna told Akshay to say 'Ganga

Narayana, Om Rama'. Akshay tried, but died before he could complete it. Suddenly, Ramakrishna began to laugh. He danced with joy. Shocking everybody he said, 'Oh! The sword is removed from the sheath. The sheath disintegrates, but the sword is eternal. Glory to Mother Kali, the creator of sheaths. Glory to Brahma who is the sword. How great is Brahman, the fire. How great is Kali, the fire's heat. How great is Kali, Mother of illusion.'

Yet, the next day, Sri Ramakrishna, who had been able to distance himself into the abstract at the death of his most beloved nephew, wept as though his heart was breaking. He spoke movingly about his grief:

Akshay died before my very eyes. But it did not affect me in the least. As I stood by and watched him die, it felt like a sword being drawn from its scabbard. I enjoyed the scene and laughed and sang and danced over it. They removed the body and cremated it. But the next day as I stood there (pointing towards the southeast veranda of his room), I felt a racking pain for Akshay's loss, as if somebody was wringing my heart like a wet towel. I wondered at the experience and thought that the Mother was teaching me a lesson. I was not much concerned even with my own body – much less with the mortal remains of a relative's. But if such was my pain at the loss of a nephew; how much more must be the grief of the other members of the family at the loss of their near and dear ones?

When Mathur Babu fell ill a few years later, Sri Ramakrishna did not visit him even once. But he knew the moment, 'Mathur was lifted into the Chariot of the Divine Mother and his spirit went to the sphere of the Devi.' Sri Ramakrishna was his oldest friend in his celestial body, all the while helping him on his last journey.

A rigid, one-dimensional man may be inflexible in his striving but a human saint is not. Holiness was not a one-sided development for Sri Ramakrishna, but a psychic whole. He was too human to embrace divinity at the expense of his humanity, too divine to act as the common maya-driven man.

Though he both laughed and cried at the death of a beloved nephew, yet there was no doubt he was more comfortable with laughter. Tears he said were a lesson from the Divine Mother on how the world suffered in the bondage of family life. Of all things that tied a man to earth, the bonds of family seemed to him the most intractable, keeping him from the knowledge of his true nature.

The sage knows we come into this world alone and leave it alone, and in addition, face all intervening trials essentially alone. Whether on some distant mountain peak or in a crowd, we are ever alone. And it is in the depths of solitude that true spiritual values are found, not in the marketplaces of the world. We confuse aloneness with loneliness, and instead of embracing our essential separation, as creative and sacred, we try to escape from it into 'I' and 'Mine'. 'This is my father, my mother, my kin, my country. My identity and fortunes are dependent on them.' In this clinging we believe we are safe. We need not find our own way. We are absolved of responsibility.

'Mother, let me remain in contact with men,' was Sri Ramakrishna's fervent prayer to Kali. 'Don't turn me into a dried- up ascetic. Don't allow my love to be swallowed up in the fires of inhuman wisdom.'

Attaining *nirvikalpa* samadhi, union with the eternal, what Hindus call Brahman and Islam calls Allah, had not slaked Sri Ramakrishna's devotional yearnings. But he had seen when passing through Dakshineswar, the results of dwelling excessively on the Infinite: desiccated sadhus like ghouls with glowing eyes, empty gourds rattling in the cosmic winds, indifferent to man.

One day a most unexpected visitor arrived at the gates of Dakshineswar, unannounced. It was Saradamani, Sri Ramakrishna's eighteen-year-old wife, along with her father. She arrived in a palanquin in a poor state of health. Life without love was inconceivable to Sri Ramakrishna: love for Brahman, the Eternal Ocean of Consciousness, for Ishwar, who is also Kali, the Divine Mother of all existence, love for man, the flesh and blood embodiment of Kali. Love was the very air he breathed.

Yet he told his devotees later, 'Do your duties, but keep your mind on God. Live with your wife and children, father and mother – and serve them. Treat them as though they are very dear to you, but know in your heart they do not belong to you.'

Sri Ramakrishna was meditating in his room when Sarada and her father came into the room. He got up instantly, helped Sarada lie on the bed, fussed over her, smoothening the pillow, making her comfortable, for she was very exhausted after the journey. Love without possessiveness? Surely a contradiction in terms? But Sri Ramakrishna demonstrated that spiritual detachment did not rule out genuine warmth and sharing. It allowed for a love that was essentially impersonal and disinterested – and for that purer, less selfish and more abundantly fruitful by virtue of this detachment.

When Saradamani was stricken with fever, Sri Ramakrishna looked after her with Hriday's help, and fed her like a child. Four years after her husband returned to Dakshineswar from Kamarpukur, Saradamani, tired of waiting to be summoned to his side, had to take the initiative. There was incessant gossip about his insanity. But remembering the gentle, considerate man who had instructed her so carefully on prayer and behaviour, she refused to believe the rumours.

With Sri Ramakrishna's loving care, food and rest, Sarada slowly gained strength. One day Sri Ramakrishna sat by her side and said, 'If only Mathur was alive he could have looked after you.' Sarada shyly replied, 'I don't need anyone else. You're looking after me so well.'

Why, it may be asked, if Sri Ramakrishna was so pleased to see his wife, had he done nothing to bring her to him? No answer can be found by applying our own standards to his actions. Sri Ramakrishna had so given himself to the will of God that it was impossible for him to make decisions beyond one minute to the next. He abhorred planning. Once, the story goes, he asked Hriday about a calf he was carrying. 'I'm taking it home,' Hriday said, 'to fatten it, so that one day it will be strong enough for the plough.' Sri Ramakrishna was so horrified he fainted. 'See how worldly men hoard for the future,' he cried, 'they have so little trust in God. Ah! This is maya!' Sri Ramakrishna believed Sarada's arrival was an indication from the Mother that they should be together. It would be his sadhana of purity.

During the next eighteen months, Sri Ramakrishna and Sarada lived together in the closest intimacy, often sleeping on the same bed. When Sarada spoke of this period in her life she described it as one of continuous ecstasy – sexless, spiritual ecstasy. Such a relationship is so unthinkable for most of us that we must take it on trust.

One day, as she sat on the ground massaging Sri Ramakrishna's feet, Sarada looked up at him and said, 'Master?' Sri Ramakrishna who was in a reverie opened his eyes and asked, 'Yes, what is it?' Sarada, lowering her eyes, replied, 'How . . . how do you think of me?' Sri Ramakrishna came back from his reverie, focussed and said, 'Think of you?' He paused, then not without difficulty replied, 'The same Mother who is in the temple . . . The same Mother who gave birth to me, and now lives in the *nahabat*. That same Mother is rubbing my feet. I see you as a form of the blissful Mother Divine.' Sarada stopped massaging, shocked by what he had said. One night, when she was asleep, Sri Ramakrishna who lay next to her woke up, watched her and then said to himself:

This, O mind, is a female body. Men look at it as an object of enjoyment, something to be prized, and they die for enjoying it. But if one possesses this body, one must remain confined within the flesh; one cannot realize God as Satchitananda. Do not, O mind, harbour one thought within and a contrary attitude without. Tell the truth whether you want the body of this woman or do you want God? If you want the body, here it is before you. Have it.

He reached out to touch her, recoiled, sat up and went into samadhi.

The choice the Master gave himself, he also offered in all fairness to his wife. 'I have learned to look on every woman as Mother,' he told her. 'That is the only idea I can have about you. But if you wish to draw me into the world as I am married to you, then I am at your service.'

However, Sarada assured him that the prospect of renouncing their spiritual intimacy and living together as ordinary man and wife was unthinkable.

Years later, the Master reflected, 'If she had not been pure, if she had lost self-control – who knows? Perhaps my own self-control would have given way, and I would have become sex-conscious. After I was married, I implored the Divine Mother to keep Sarada's consciousness absolutely free from lust. Now after living with Sarada all that time, I knew the Mother had granted my prayer.'

Sarada Devi's greatest contribution to mankind, it might be said, was Sri Ramakrishna himself!

Once, Sarada who had otherwise accepted a life of celibacy, hesitatingly and unhappily told Sri Ramakrishna, 'I only sometimes think . . . I will . . . never have children of my own.'

Sri Ramakrishna assured her and said, 'Look here, you will be Mother not to five or six, but to hundreds of thousands. The world will call you Mother . . . That is what you were born for.' Sarada looked up at him with surprise and disbelief, but slowly settled down as understanding dawned on her.

'I have a human body,' Sri Ramakrishna told his disciples later. 'If I were to say, "I have conquered lust", it would be said in pride, and I would fall. I accept the existence of lust without shame and guilt. And let it pass. As I do so many disturbing behaviours of the body . . .'

Sri Ramakrishna did not hold that sex is sinful – sexuality is part of maya as is any manifestation of nature. In tantra, which Sri Ramakrishna had practised intimately under the guidance of Brahmani, sex is sacred, symbolic of the union of Shiva and Shakti, Spirit and Matter, from which the universe in its multitudinous variations is born. But sex thrives in duality, the sense of separation and incompleteness that is diametrically opposed to the consciousness of union that is the touchstone of the spiritual.

Having fallen into incompletion, man hungers for a union that will make him whole. But the promise of union through sex is a mirage. Energies burned out without attaining the goal of completion through sex, we then begin to search beyond the physical for a deeper meaning. Science, philosophy, art – civilization itself, are products of this groping search for light.

Sri Ramakrishna knew that an attempt to gain fulfilment at the level of the body or of the mind alone is futile. Mind and body are themselves only fragments of a vaster, more awesome whole that we sense only fleetingly at the edges of consciousness. We call this feeling of completion God, or the Divine Mother, or eternity, or infinity, or Allah. And man knows that nothing short of this union will satisfy the deepest yearnings of his soul.

Once, late at night, Sri Ramakrishna was in his room in deep samadhi. Sarada suddenly awakened and found him sitting soundless and still. Seeing his stillness, she got worried and tried to shake him.

Unable to move him she went to the door and called out to Hriday. Hriday came in and chanted mantras in Sri Ramakrishna's ears till he opened his eyes. Sarada was relieved. The next morning Sarada told Sri Ramakrishna, 'I could not move you, Master. You were in samadhi so long. Longer than usual. Last night I was so frightened.'

Sri Ramakrishna answered gently, 'I cannot control my samadhi. And you should sleep undisturbed. Perhaps it is best if you sleep in the *nahabat*, above, with Mother.'

Chandra Devi, Sri Ramakrishna's mother, who had moved into the cramped room on the first floor of the Music Tower, was only too glad to have her daughter-in-law live below. Sarada, who believed with a certain verisimilitude, as Hindu women of the time were taught, that her husband was God, lived there each time she visited Dakshineswar. She prepared meals for Sri Ramakrishna's delicate stomach and nourished her own spiritual evolution.

The holy fire of God-inebriation had burned in Sri Ramakrishna for twelve years and kept him engaged in practices of spiritual moods without rest. He had long ago sacrificed all desirable things of the world: wealth, honour, fame . . . his heart, mind, intellect, memory. The only thing that remained was the desire to see the Mother of the universe. This too he sacrificed.

A few months after Sarada Devi's arrival, on the night of the new moon reserved for the worship of Kali, Sri Ramakrishna placed on the seat the living image – Saradamani herself – instead of an image of the deity, and thereby symbolically elevated all Indian women to the pedestal of their former glory.

As part of the ritual of the Shodasi Puja, Sri Ramakrishna called out to Sarada who opened her eyes with difficulty, stood up with the help of the priest and came forward. Sri Ramakrishna took her by the hand, sat her on the pedestal, sprinkled holy water from a pitcher and chanted, '*O Lady, Mother Tripurasundari, O Mistress of all Power. Open the door to perfection. Purify the body of this woman. Manifest yourself in her and be beneficent.*' Sri Ramakrishna performed *nyasa* of mantras. He made sixteen ritual offerings including earth, ether, fire and water and put food in Sarada's mouth.

The worshipper and the worshipped went into a deep samadhi and their souls united in the transcendental plane. After several hours, Sri Ramakrishna came down to the relative plane, sang a hymn to the great Goddess, and surrendered – at the feet of the living image – himself, his rosary, the fruit of his lifelong sadhana and said:

> *O auspiciousness of all auspicious things.*
> *O door of all actions.*
> *O refuge.*
> *Three-eyed-one.*
> *O spouse of Shiva,*
> *O Narayani.*
> *I bow down to thee.*
> *I bow down to thee.*

In tantra this is known as the Sodashi Puja, the adoration of the Divine Virgin – a rarely performed tantric ritual.

Sri Ramakrishna realized the significance of the great statement of the Upanishad: 'O Lord, Thou art the woman, Thou art the man; Thou art the boy, Thou art the girl; Thou art the old, tottering on their crutches; Thou pervades the universe in its multiple forms.'

Sri Ramakrishna admitted the great value of marriage in man's spiritual evolution, and by adhering to his monastic vows he demonstrated the imperative necessity of self-control, purity and continence, in the realization of God. By his unique relationship with his wife, he proved that husband and wife can live together as spiritual companions. Thus, life is a synthesis of the ways of life of a householder and a monk.

Eight years later, in November 1874, Sri Ramakrishna was seized with an irresistible desire to learn more about the Christian religion. Therefore, soon after Sarada left for Kamarpukur, Sri Ramakrishna visited a neighbour, Shambhucharan Mallick. Gregarious, well read, devout and generous, he had virtually taken over from Mathur, as provider of Sri Ramakrishna's physical needs. Shambhucharan was catholic in his tastes – he read all the religious treatises with equal enthusiasm, and read excerpts from the Bible to his Master.

Sri Ramakrishna became fascinated by the life and teachings of Jesus. One day while he was seated in the parlour of Mallick's garden house at Dakshineswar, his eyes became fixed on a painting of the Madonna and Child. He watched it intently and was unable to tear his eyes away from it. Gradually, he became overwhelmed with emotion. The figures in the picture took on life, and the rays of light emanating from them entered his soul. The effect of this experience was stronger than that of the vision of Muhammad. In dismay he cried out, 'O Mother! What are you doing to me?' And breaking through the barriers of creed and religion, he entered a new realm of ecstasy. Jesus Christ possessed his soul.

For three days he did not set foot inside the Kali temple. On the fourth afternoon, while he was meditating in Panchavati, he saw a tall fair man – serene, handsome, with a slightly semitic nose and light coloured eyes, dressed in a long white robe, coming gracefully towards him. A voice rang out in the depths of Sri Ramakrishna's soul: 'Behold the Christ, who shed His heart's blood for the redemption of the world, who suffered a sea of anguish for love of man. It is He, the Master Yogi, who is in eternal union with God. It is Jesus, love incarnate.' The Son of Man embraced the Son of the Divine Mother and merged in Him. Sri Ramakrishna realized his identity with Christ, as he had already realized his identity with Kali, Rama, Hanuman, Radha, Krishna and Brahman with attributes. Thus he experienced the truth that Christianity too, was a path leading to God-consciousness. Till the last moment of his life, he believed that Christ was an incarnation of God. But Christ, for him, was not the *only* incarnation; there were others – Buddha, Krishna and many others.

Eight years after engaging in the sadhanas of the Islamic faith, just as unexpectedly, Sri Ramakrishna experienced the *dvaitic* form of Christ – as he had Muhammad and Ma Kali – dissolve into the *advaitic* source of all creation as he went again into *nirvikalpa* samadhi.

All paths he declared later in his most illuminating and inspired lectures, lead to the same source. He said this with complete conviction. His devotions led him to an experience of the Buddha and Jain Mahavira as avatars, of the sage-king Janaka and the Sikh Gurus.

One day the news arrived from Kamarpukur that yet another relative had died. Sri Ramakrishna conveyed the news to his mother with tearful eyes, 'Mother, Rameshwar Dada died in Kamarpukur. Ramlal took Rameshwar Dada's ashes to Calcutta and scattered them in the Ganga.' Chandra Devi, herself old and fragile, told Sri Ramakrishna, 'My heart is wrenched, and my son . . . my second son . . . has gone to his Divine Mother.' She then turned to Sri Ramakrishna and consoled him, 'Don't weep, Gadai. What is the use of grieving? This world is transitory. Everyone passes out of it some day . . .' Sri Ramakrishna was surprised by her words. He smiled and touched her feet, saying, 'Of what use is it to assume a human body if its purpose of attaining God is not achieved. The Divine Mother has tuned you to a high pitch like a finely tuned instrument, my Mother, so worldly sorrows cannot touch you any more. I am no longer anxious about you.'

Three years later, Chandra Devi herself died at the age of ninety-four. As a sannyasi, whose life was based on the assertion that the world and all its changes are unreal, Sri Ramakrishna was unable to take part in religious ceremonies related to birth, marriage and death. But ever torn between humanity and divinity, Sri Ramakrishna felt guilty that he had not honoured his mother by the ritual proper to a son. So he tried to perform the *tarpana* after the funeral rites were over.

Along with the pandit, Sri Ramakrishna began to perform his mother's death rituals. Every time the pandit tried to pour some water into Sri Ramakrishna's cupped hands, they trembled and the water trickled down. This was repeated again and again. Sri Ramakrishna felt very unhappy and cried out, 'O Divine Mother, what have you done to me? I cannot even offer *tarpana* to my mother's departed spirit. O Mother forgive me.'

The pandit, seeing his dismay, told Sri Ramakrishna, 'My son, do not reproach yourself. The scriptures state that when a man has reached a high level of spiritual development, his actions drop off and he is unable to fulfil the prescribed rituals, even if he earnestly wants to. There is no sin in this.'

This state perhaps marked the climax of Sri Ramakrishna's sadhana, the period of his spiritual discipline. As a result of his long and difficult journey, he had arrived at insights and realizations; conclusions regarding himself and spirituality in general that could now be more formally ascribed to him and represented much that he would articulate himself.

He was an incarnation of God, a person whose spiritual experiences were for the benefit of humanity. An ordinary man struggles his entire life to realize one or two facets of God, but Sri Ramakrishna had, within a few years, realized God in all His facets. Second, he knew that he had always been a free soul and that the various disciplines which he passed through were not necessary for his own liberation, but solely for the benefit of others. Thus, the terms liberation and bondage were not applicable to him. As long as there are human beings who consider themselves bound, God must come down to earth as an incarnation to free them from bondage. Third, he came to foresee the time of his death. His words came true in the future. He also arrived at some conclusions regarding spirituality.

He was firmly convinced that all religions are true. Every system of doctrine represents a path to God. He had followed all the main paths and all had led him to the same goal. He was the first religious prophet in recorded history to preach the harmony of religions.

Second, he perceived the three great schools of thought – known as Dualism, Qualified Non-dualism and Absolute Non-dualism – that is, *Dvaita, Visishtadvaita*, and *Advaita* – to represent the three stages in man's progress towards the attainment of ultimate reality. They were not contradictory but complementary and suited to different temperaments. For the ordinary man with a strong attachment to the senses, a dualistic form of religion, prescribing a certain amount of material support like music and other symbols, is useful. A man of God-realization transcends the idea of worldly duties, but the ordinary mortal must perform his duties, striving to remain unattached and simultaneously surrendering the results to God. The mind can comprehend and describe the range of thought and experience up to the *Visishtadvaita*, but no further. *Advaita*, the last stage in spiritual experience, is something to be felt in samadhi only, for it transcends mind and speech. From that point, the Absolute and its manifestation, both are equally real. Everything is essentially spirit; the difference is only in form.

Third, Sri Ramakrishna realized the wish of the Divine Mother – that through him She wanted to found an Order, comprising those who would uphold the universal doctrines illustrated in his life.

Fourth, his spiritual insight told him that those who were living their last birth on the mortal plane of existence and those who had sincerely called the Lord even once in their lives would eventually come to him.

During this period, Sri Ramakrishna suffered several bereavements. The first was the death of his nephew Akshay. In 1871, Mathur died, and about five years later Shambhucharan Mallick – who, after Mathur's death, took care of Sri Ramakrishna's physical comfort. In 1873, his elder brother Rameshwar passed away, and in 1876, his beloved mother. These bereavements left their imprint on Sri Ramakrishna's tender human heart, albeit he realized the immortality of the soul and the illusoriness of birth and death.

In March 1875, about a year before the death of his mother, Sri Ramakrishna met the Brahmo Samaj leader Keshab Chandra Sen, who was to inspire and impact Vivekananda's search. The meeting was a momentous event for both. Here for the first time, Sri Ramakrishna came into contact with a worthy representative of modern India.

Another phase of Sri Ramakrishna's life was born. Every event opened out to a new one. Till now, the world knew Sri Ramakrishna as a crazy man with all kinds of visions and experiences to which only he was testimony. What relevance these experiences had was yet to be seen. Sri Ramakrishna now looked forward to his spiritual children. In anticipation he said, 'O my children, where are you? Come! Why haven't you come yet? My soul is wrung out like a wet towel waiting for you. Mother, you told me that my devotees would come . . . Why have they not come Mother? What will this life have been worth if they do not come? What will my life have been worth then?'

Sri Ramakrishna walking towards Kali temple.
(*Sketch by* Nandlal Bose)

Five

The Mission

Who knows what Kali is.
The six philosophies cannot explain her . . .

Raja Rammohan Roy

$\mathcal{S}$ri Ramakrishna continued his evolution in human form with myriad insights and experiences. His was not a single transforming moment of enlightenment, but a continuing sadhana along the different paths available to humankind. This was a time when parts of urban Bengal came under the influence of the imperial British intellectual traditions.

In 1774, a boy was born to an orthodox, aristocratic Bengali Brahmin family, that, at the age of sixteen, he offended mightily by publishing a book against image worship. This boy was Rammohan Roy. Like many upper-class Indians educated by the British, he had misunderstood the mind of India at its most fundamental.

English missionaries, their ignorance of the Vedas inexhaustible, held that 'Hinduism' was a primitive polytheistic tangle of cults and idolatry, far inferior to the teachings of Jesus Christ.

These intellectual young men of India, uncomfortably straddling two cultures, aped their conquerors indiscriminately. As the conquered do, they absorbed their values, cloned themselves on their fashions and hoped to acquire, thereby, the powers of the 'superior race'. Beset by a severe inferiority complex engendered by their supercilious masters, they were despised by the British because of their hopeless efforts at imitation, and condemned by orthodox Hindus as traitors to the traditions of their people.

Rammohan Roy had shown great sympathy for Islam and Christianity. He went to Tibet in search of the Buddhist mysteries. He extracted from Christianity its ethical system, but rejected the divinity of Christ as he denied the Hindu incarnation. The religion of Islam influenced him to a great extent in the formulation of his monotheistic doctrines. But he always went back to the Vedas for his spiritual inspiration.

The founder of the Brahmo movement and the Brahmo Samaj (1828), Raja Rammohan Roy (given the title of Raja by the Emperor of Delhi in 1830) was dedicated to the 'worship and adoration of the Eternal, the Unsearchable, the Immutable Being, who is the Author and Preserver of the Universe'. The Samaj was open to all without distinction of colour, creed, caste, nation or religion.

But Raja Rammohan Roy had an enquiring, intelligent mind. While in alliance with British colonial authorities and Indian free thinkers, he challenged the ossified, misunderstood, misused Hindu practices of sati, caste and the oppressive illiteracy of women, yet he believed India should return to the original purity of ancient Vedic concepts of virtuous behaviour and the worship of the Eternal.

However, the need to be accepted by the British was such that the rituals of the Brahmo Samaj sounded almost like a Protestant church service, thereby alienating the majority of Indians who needed the colour and variety of their own traditions.

While Sri Ramakrishna did not meet Raja Rammohan Roy, who died on a visit to England, he did briefly meet his successor, Devendranath Tagore, father of the redoubtable Rabindranath – the icon of modern Bengali culture. Raja Rammohan Roy's Brahmo Samaj, while carrying in its centre the essential spark of Indian mysticism, swung West in many of its forms and beliefs. But Devendranath Tagore's Brahmo Samaj swung East, drawing its inspiration from the Hindu scriptures, fighting to keep elements of Christianity out.

One fine day, Sri Ramakrishna was invited to Devendranath Tagore's house where he went with Hriday. It was a congregation of men and suddenly Sri Ramakrishna spotted one man in the crowd and said, 'That man there, he is the only one amongst these Brahmos who has achieved a state of true meditation. Who is he?' Hriday looked around and answered, 'His name is Keshab Chandra Sen.' At that moment Devendranath Tagore approached Sri Ramakrishna, touched his feet and welcomed him 'I am honoured, Master, that you have come to my humble home.' Much to everyone's surprise, Sri Ramakrishna said to Devendra Babu, 'You are known to be spiritually advanced. Would you show me your chest?' Devendranath smiled, picked up his shirt and bared his chest. Sri Ramakrishna leaned forward and saw the flushed chest and said, 'Yes, yes, good. The flush shows that you have been in deep and prolonged meditation.' Devendranath replied that he believed that the world is like a chandelier in which every living creature is a light. God created man to proclaim his glory. If there were no lights in the chandelier, all was darkness. Sri Ramakrishna with much excitement exclaimed, 'Yes! Yes! I have seen this vision too.'

Powerfully influenced by the life of Jesus Christ, Keshab Chandra Sen later split from Devendranath Tagore to form the Brahmo Samaj of India that swung once again on a pendulum towards the West. Keshab remained the leader of the Brahmo Samaj, one of the two great movements that during the latter half of the nineteenth century played an important part in shaping the course of Indian renaissance.

His was a complex nature. When passing through a great moral crisis, Keshab spent much of his time in solitude and felt that he heard the voice of God. When a devotional form of worship was introduced into the Brahmo Samaj, he spent hours singing *kirtan* or hymns with his followers. In 1870 he visited England and impressed the English people with his musical voice, his simple English, and his spiritual fervour. There, Queen

Victoria entertained him. Returning to India, he founded centres of the Brahmo Samaj in various parts of the country. Not unlike a professor of comparative religion in a European university, he began to discover, about the time of his first contact with Sri Ramakrishna, the harmony of religions. He became sympathetic towards the Hindu gods and goddesses, explaining them in a liberal fashion. Further, he believed that he was called by God to dictate to the world God's newly revealed law, the New Dispensation, the Navavidhan.

Keshab Chandra Sen was very passionate about his ideas and spoke eloquently in public. He said things like: 'Who rules India? . . . What power is it that sways the destiny of this land? . . . It is not the glittering bayonet, the thundering cannon that make the people of India loyal. No. It is spiritual influence, it is moral suasion. Our hearts have been touched and subjugated by a superior power and the power is not the British government; it is Jesus Christ.' And the missionaries would smile and nod to each other satisfied. With genuine fervour, Keshab Chandra Sen continued:

> My thoughts are never far from God; my life is a constant prayer. I am a born disciple. All objects are my Masters, I learn from everything. By my own understanding, I have found all truths are common to all, for all are of God. Truth is no more European than Asiatic. No more yours than mine.

It was the complex, enigmatic, searching Keshab Chandra Sen, full of contradictions, who introduced the Calcutta intelligentsia to Sri Ramakrishna. And it was from the ranks of the Westernized Bengali intellectuals of the Brahmo Samaj, alienated from their own people, but yearning for a lifeline to spiritual values that had sustained their countrymen over the centuries, that Sri Ramakrishna's most doubting, contentious, fractious, argumentative and ultimately devoted and longed-for disciples would come.

It was at this time that Hriday went to Keshab Chandra Sen and requested, 'My uncle Sri Ramakrishna is a great lover of God. He has heard you are also a great devotee and has come to listen to you talk on God's divine glory. May I bring him to you?' Keshab Sen nodded and said, 'By all means. We have heard of him.'

Keshab Chandra Sen and Sri Ramakrishna met for the first time in the garden house of Jaygopal Sen at Belgharia, a few miles from Dakshineswar, where the great Brahmo leader stayed with some of his disciples.

Dressed in a red-bordered dhoti, one end of which was carelessly thrown over his left shoulder, Sri Ramakrishna arrived at Jaygopal's house accompanied by Hriday. No one noticed the unostentatious visitor. Finally, the Master approached Keshab. 'People tell me you have seen God; so I have come to hear about God from you.' A magnificent conversation followed. The Master sang a thrilling song about Kali and went into samadhi. When Hriday uttered the sacred 'Om' in his ears, he gradually came back to consciousness, but his face still radiated a divine brilliance. Keshab and his followers were amazed.

The contrast between Sri Ramakrishna and the Brahmo devotees was very interesting. There sat this small man, thin and extremely delicate, but his eyes were illuminated with an inner light and good humour flirted around the corners of his mouth. Though he spoke in Bangla, with a slight, delightful stammer; his words held men enthralled by their wealth of spiritual experience, their inexhaustible store of simile and metaphor, their power of observation, their bright and subtle humour, their wonderful catholicity and their ceaseless flow of wisdom. All around him now were the sophisticated men of Bengal, the best products of Western education, with Keshab, the idol of young Bengal, as their leader.

Sri Ramakrishna humbly asked, 'Is it true that you had a vision of God? Will you tell me of your experience?' Keshab Sen politely answered, 'We would rather listen to you, Sir. We learn from all who care to teach.' Sri Ramakrishna began to sing . . .

Who knows what Kali is.
The six philosophies cannot explain her . . .

Some of Keshab Sen's followers ridiculed Sri Ramakrishna. Some said, 'He's sick in his head' and some said that it was a trick. Addressing the sceptic members, Sri Ramakrishna related this story:

A man told his friends he saw a red chameleon under a tree. One said: 'No. I saw it earlier, it was green.' Another went to look and returned saying: 'You are both fools; its neither; it's blue.' They began to fight. Then a fourth man, who had been listening quietly, said: 'I live under the tree; the chameleon is red; it is also blue and also green and sometimes it is other colours and sometimes no colour at all.'

Slowly, the Brahmos began to pay attention and listened to Sri Ramakrishna who explained that each devotee looked at Brahman with his own vision:

Therefore, Brahman is one, but also many. There are many ways of realizing God . . . you can enter a room by the door, through the window or through the chimney. You cannot grasp God with your intellect; the intellect is limited, merely a tool. The source of being is beyond thought – for thought is a Doing. You can only grasp the Eternal with all your soul, through devotion. If you accept the existence of

Brahman, you must also accept the existence of the creative power of Brahman. Brahman and his power are one and the same – do you agree?

Keshab Chandra Sen agreed and said, 'Yes.' Sri Ramakrishna continued. 'So the Divine Word that comes from the power of Brahman – and is written in the scriptures – and Brahman is also one?'

Keshab Sen was speechless and agreed again, though reluctantly.

Sri Ramakrishna continued. 'And the devotee who is created by the power of Brahman and listens to the Divine Word and the Divine Word are also One?'

Keshab Sen listened in silence.

Sri Ramakrishna further said, 'So three entities: the Lord, the Word and the Devotee are One, are they not? The three is One the One is the three.'

Finally, Keshab Sen could not take any more of what Sri Ramakrishna was saying, something which was contrary to his philosophy. 'Master . . . I . . . can't accept now all that you've said. But there seems to be something . . . I'll have to think it over.'

Sri Ramakrishna's eyes twinkled and much to the discomfort of the Brahmos he added, 'Your tail has fallen off. Before the tadpole can move on land as a frog, its tail must fall off. It is preferable, is it not, to move on both land and in water?' After the exchange of words and opinions the congregation got up to leave. Sri Ramakrishna along with Hriday moved towards the gates, escorted by Keshab Sen.

In many respects, Sri Ramakrishna and Keshab Chandra Sen were poles apart, though there remained an irresistible inner attraction, which made them intimate friends in the near future.

The Master realized God as pure spirit and consciousness, but he believed in various forms of God as well. Keshab on the other hand, regarded image worship as idolatry and gave allegorical explanations of the Hindu deities. Keshab's skills lay in oration, writing books and magazine articles. Sri Ramakrishna had a horror of lecturing and barely knew how to write even his own name. Keshab's fame spread far and wide, it even reached the distant shores of England. The Master led a secluded life in the village of Dakshineswar. Keshab emphasized social reforms for India's regeneration. But for Sri Ramakrishna realization of God was the only goal of life. Keshab was a householder and took real interest in the welfare of his children, whereas Sri Ramakrishna was a Paramahamsa and completely indifferent to worldly life. Yet, as their acquaintance grew into friendship, Sri Ramakrishna and Keshab regarded each other with great love and respect.

Keshab Chandra, the subtle, refined, sophisticate was hooked by a humble, earthy village priest. Keshab's religion was an abstraction, Sri Ramakrishna's of concrete spiritual experience. On the surface, Keshab's rationalistic conception of religion had little in common with Sri Ramakrishna's rainbow profusions of gods, sadhanas and parables. But underneath the surface duality of style, powerfully, invisibly, ran a shared tide of yearning for the Infinite that marked them as brothers.

Keshab was sharp and discriminating, Sri Ramakrishna broad-minded and tolerant. In Sri Ramakrishna's simplicity, calm and self-assurance, Keshab found a soothing complement to his tortured over-sophistication. He came to Dakshineswar frequently thereafter, delighting in the powerful sense of God's presence that recharged his batteries. It became so that a few days away from Dakshineswar, and Keshab became restless for Sri Ramakrishna's company. The same pattern followed for many Brahmos who eventually formed the inner circle of Sri Ramakrishna's devotees.

Years later, at the news of Keshab's death, the Master felt as if half his body had become paralyzed. Keshab's concepts of the harmony of religions and the Motherhood of God were deepened and enriched by his contact with Sri Ramakrishna.

During one conversation between Sri Ramakrishna and Keshab Sen, Sri Ramakrishna said:

> You wish to be strict and partial. For myself, I have a burning desire to worship the Lord in every way I can, but my heart's desire has never been satisfied. I long to worship Him with offerings of flowers and fruit, to repeat His holy name in solitude, to sing His hymns, to dance in the joy of the Lord. Those who believe the Lord is without form attain Him just as those who believe He has a form. The only two essentials are faith and surrender.
>
> Someone once read to me a book of the Christians. It talked of nothing but sin, sin and sin. Sin is the only thing one hears in your Brahmo Samaj, too. The wretch who says day and night I am a sinner, I am a sinner, ends up becoming one. You should have such a burning faith in God so as to say: 'What? I have repeated the name of God. Can sin still cling to me?' If a man repeats the Divine name, everything becomes pure. Why should one dwell on sin and hell and such things?
>
> Truth is of two kinds: That which is verifiable through the senses – scientific knowledge, confined to the world of transient matter. And that which is perceivable by subtle intuition arising from yoga – Vedic knowledge, that is eternal, not confined to time and place. The Creator itself creates, maintains and destroys the world with Vedic knowledge.

Until a man's life opens out to Vedic knowledge, religion is to him a meaningless word. The Vedas concern work and knowledge. Work exists in the realm of the material world, in maya. Knowledge is eternal. This is the Vedanta. With the degradation of life, the Vedanta was taught in gross forms for the consumption of weak minds. It was separated and divided by sects and denominations that turned against each other and converted this land of religion into a veritable hell. It was the religious disciples of Sri Ramakrishna who demonstrated the fundamental unity of all the world's religions.

If Sri Ramakrishna's early life was a process of purification, the stage of samadhis was a process of illumination. The process of experiencing the harmonies of all religions was the punitive stage of his life. Then he entered a stage of dispersal as he began to share generously of his experiences and insights. Many scholars and devotees came to him and many he sought out. He tried to meet as many as he could of both those who took the route of learning, of discrimination, and those who took the route of devotion. But none had yet come to him as disciples.

It was not till twelve years after he had attained *nirvikalpa* samadhi, when he had felt the first stirrings of longing for those who might understand his experience, that his disciples, his sons of the spirit, began to arrive and the path to his door was trodden by the modern young Brahmos of Bengal, steeped in intellectual discrimination.

Surely the Divine Mother had arranged things well, for it is in conflict, in testing, in the clash of opposites, in the collision of wills and minds that the truth appears. Truth with roots so deep in the eternal, so as to seep down the generations, as Sri Ramakrishna's countrymen cycle back to the same point on a different plane: pulled towards a Western concept of progress, education and duality, longing for union, for lost links to their own roots of the spirit.

One day, when Sri Ramakrishna was in his room meditating, Manmohan Mitra and Ramachandra Dutta arrived at his door. Sri Ramakrishna rose and opened it on hearing the knock. The two men ignored Sri Ramakrishna and looked around for the saint. After realizing their folly they fell at his feet.

They were the first recruits to what became Sri Ramakrishna's inner circle. A doctor by profession, Ramachandra Dutta and his cousin Manmohan Mitra were both members of the Brahmo Samaj, which they had joined in their search for meaning in a world seemingly adrift, cut away from tradition. But they had become disillusioned with sterile platitudes and empty rituals.

Sri Ramakrishna asked them, 'Do you believe in God? Do you yearn to know him?' Manmohan Mitra honestly said, 'We believe in the Brahmo philosophy to be of service to others . . . but as for God . . .' Ramachandra Dutta added, 'We are materialists, Sir. What we can't make out with our senses has no meaning for us.' Sri Ramakrishna was amused and said, 'You think God can be realized through the senses?' and looked at them steadily, smiling wryly. 'But would you have come all the way here if you were not restless to realize him? Would you not be indulging in what your friends call fun?' Ramachandra Dutta asked, 'Does God really exist?' Sri Ramakrishna replied, 'Of course He exists. Just as the stars exist during the day – although you don't see them. Just looking at milk you cannot see butter. To get butter you have to churn the milk in a cool place. To see God you have to practise mental disciplines.'

They came to Dakshineswar out of curiosity, well-armed with a healthy scepticism against matted hair, loincloths, tridents and hollow, fanatical eyes. But Sri Ramakrishna did not fit their stereotypes. Now, they were drawn by his cheerful, buoyant enthusiasm, his practical approach towards spirituality, by the fact that he never fell back on Sanskrit *shlokas* to prop up his discourses, but spoke simply out of his own experiences. Soon, almost despite themselves, they were regular Sunday visitors. One day Sri Ramakrishna, Ramachandra Dutt and Manmohan Mitra were sitting together when Sri Ramakrishna asked, 'What do you see when you look at me?'

Ramachandra Dutta answered, 'I think you are Sri Chaitanya.'

'Bhairavi used to say that. Yet I see you doubt me?' said Sri Ramakrishna.

The process through which Ramachandra Dutta stepped off his pedestal of intellect was long and tortuous, testing his sanity, faith and commitment and that of his family.

One day, as Ramachandra Dutta was reading a book by a Western philosopher, he saw Sri Ramakrishna's face on the page and heard his words as if he was there: 'God is your father and mother. Call out to him sincerely and he will come.' Closing the book with a bang, he went out of the room and walked restlessly on the streets. He felt anguished and told Manmohan Mitra his experience. 'I'm torn between this and that. My wife or sannyas. My scientific education or God. Nothing satisfies me. Nothing gives me peace.' Manmohan Mitra, also in the same state of mind, said, 'The Master says my capacity for devotion is unequalled. I wonder what that means.' Both went to the Master and Ramachandra Dutta fell at his feet, imploring, 'I beg you. Initiate me into sannyas. Of what use is the world without God.'

Sri Ramakrishna advised him that nothing should be done on the spur of the moment. 'What will you gain by renouncing the world? Family life is a fortress. You will be able to renounce the world only when you give three-quarters of your mind to God.'

The next morning, Ramachandra Dutta returned to the Master full of self-pity and extreme melancholy and said, 'I feel like a stray dog without a leash. Help me find peace, Master.' Sri Ramakrishna curtly told him that he could do nothing. It all depended on the will of God. Ramachandra Dutta pleaded, 'All this time I've looked to you for help. How can you treat me like this?' And the Master responded neutrally, 'I owe you nothing. You may come here if you like. If not, don't.'

Ramakrishna had a unique method of teaching. Ramachandra Dutta, whom he refused to help despite what seemed like his desperation to any onlooker, was served what felt like harsh treatment. Obviously, Ramakrishna had other plans in his mind and perhaps Ramachandra Dutta at that time was not prepared for any lessons, however interested and keen he may have appeared. He had to work hard to earn his grace. And the time had obviously come, so it was that the miserly and doubting Ramachandra Dutta learned to serve, to give generously and to have faith.

Eventually, one day Sri Ramakrishna came out of his room and asked him, 'What do you want? Ask me for whatever you want.' Ramachandra Dutta was most unprepared for this grace and in an undecided mind simply answered with emotion, 'Lord, I do not know what to ask of you. Wealth and fame have no meaning. Give me what you want . . . What you think I ought to have. Your will is greater than mine.' Ramakrishna went into samadhi and extended his hand and said, 'You dreamed I gave you a mantra. Give it back to me, it does not belong to you.' Ramachandra Dutta fell at the Master's feet. Ramakrishna touched him on his head with his toe and said, 'Look at me and see what you wish.' The obviously transformed Ramachandra Dutta had no words, but suddenly radiated an expression of bliss.

Totally untouched by the idea of being a teacher, the Master remained a willing instrument in the hand of God, the child of the Divine Mother. He said that three ideas – that he was a guru, a father and a Master – pricked his flesh like thorns. Yet, he was an extraordinary teacher. He influenced his disciples subtly and not by actions or words. He never claimed to be the founder of a religion or the organizer of a sect. Yet, he was a religious dynamo. He was the verifier of all religions and creeds. He was like an expert gardener who prepares the soil and removes the weeds, knowing that the plants will grow because of the inherent potential of the seeds, producing appropriate flowers and fruit. He had the unusual power of knowing the devotees' minds, even what lay in their innermost souls, at first glance. He accepted disciples with the full knowledge of their past tendencies and future possibilities. The life of evil did not frighten him, nor did religious squeamishness raise anybody in his estimation. He saw in everything the unerring touch of the Divine Mother. Even the light that leads astray was to him the light from God.

To those who became his intimate disciples, the Master was a friend, companion and playmate. Even the chores of religious discipline were lightened in his presence. The devotees were so inebriated with pure joy in his company that they had no time to ask themselves whether he was an incarnation, a perfect soul or a yogi. His very presence was a great lesson; words were superfluous. In later years, his disciples remarked that while they were with him they regarded him as a comrade, but afterwards trembled to think of their frivolities in the presence of such a great Master. They had convincing proof that the Master could, by his mere wish, kindle in their hearts the love of God and His vision.

Amidst all the fun and frolic, merriment and frivolity, he always kept before his disciples the shining ideal of God-consciousness and the path of renunciation. He prescribed steep ascents or grades according to the powers of the climber. That is, he gave lessons according to the capability of the individuals. Not too tough and not too easy either. Just as much pressure as they could handle. He permitted no compromise with the basic principles of purity. An aspirant had to keep his body, mind, senses and soul unblemished. They had to have a sincere love for God and an ever-mounting spirit of yearning. The rest would be done by the Mother.

The next person to arrive was Suresh Mitra, a friend of Ramachandra Dutta, who had a well-paying job with a British firm in Calcutta. When he came to see that peculiar Holy Man of Dakshineswar, the one his friend Dutta always talked about, he had no desire to serve, other than to give money occasionally to the poor.

Soon to become a beloved disciple, he was often addressed as Surendra by the Master. Like many other educated young men of the time, he prided himself on his atheism and led a bohemian life. He was addicted to drinking and cherished an exaggerated notion about man's free will. A victim of mental depression, he was brought to Sri Ramakrishna by Ramachandra Dutta. When he heard the Master asking a disciple to practise the virtue of self-surrender to God, he was greatly impressed. But though he tried, thenceforth, to do so, he was unable to give up his old associates or his drinking habits. One day the Master said in his presence, 'Well, when a man goes to an undesirable place, why doesn't he take the Divine Mother with him?' To Surendra himself, Sri Ramakrishna said:

Why should you drink wine as wine? Offer it to Kali, and then take it as Her prasad, as consecrated drink. But see that you don't become intoxicated; you must not reel and your thoughts must not wander. At first you will feel ordinary excitement, but soon you will experience spiritual exaltation.

Slowly, Surendra's entire life changed. The Master designated him as one of those commissioned by the Divine Mother to defray a great part of his expenses. Surendra's purse was always open for the Master's comfort.

Gradually, other Brahmo leaders began to feel Sri Ramakrishna's influence. But they were by no means uncritical admirers of the Master. They particularly disapproved of his ascetic renunciation and condemnation of 'women and gold', because they measured him according to their own ideals of the householder's life. Some could not understand why he went into samadhi and described it as a nervous malady. Yet they were unable to resist his magnetic personality.

Among the Brahmo leaders who knew the master closely were Pratap Chandra Mazumdar, Vijaykrishna Goswami, Trailokyanath Sanyal and Shivanath Shastri.

Shivanath was very impressed by the Master's utter simplicity and abhorrence of praise. One day, he was seated with Sri Ramakrishna in the latter's room when several rich men of Calcutta arrived. The Master left the room for a few minutes. In the meantime, Hriday began to describe his samadhi to the visitors. The last few words caught the Master's ear. He admonished Hriday, 'Why must you extol me thus, before these rich men? You have seen their costly apparel and their gold watches and chains, and your object is to get as much money as you can from them. What do I care about what they think of me?' Turning to the visitors, Sri Ramakrishna said:

No, my friends, what he has told you about me is not true. It wasn't love of God that made me absorbed in God and indifferent to external life. I became positively insane for some time. The sadhus who frequented this temple told me to practise many things. I tried to follow them and consequently my austerities drove me to insanity.

This is a quotation from one of Shivanath's books. He took the Master's words literally and failed to understand their real import.

Shivanath vehemently criticized the Master for his otherworldly attitude towards his wife. He wrote:

Ramakrishna was practically separated from his wife, who lived in her village home. One day, when I was complaining to some friends about the virtual widowhood of his wife, he drew me to one side and whispered in my ear: 'Why do you complain? It is no longer possible; it is all dead and gone.' Another day, as I was inveighing against this part of his teaching, and also declaring that our programme of work in the Brahmo Samaj includes women and that ours is a social and domestic religion, he became very excited, as was his way when anything against his settled conviction was asserted – a trait we so much liked in him – and exclaimed, 'Go, thou fool, go and perish in the pit that your women will dig for you.' Then he glared at me and said: 'What does a gardener do with a young plant? Does he not surround it with a fence, to protect it from goats and cattle? And when the young plant has grown up into a tree and it can no longer be injured by cattle, does he not remove the fence and let the tree grow freely?' I replied, 'Yes, that is the custom with gardeners.' Then he remarked, 'Do the same in your spiritual life; become strong, be full-grown; then you may seek them.' To which I replied, 'I don't agree with you in thinking that women's work is like that of cattle, destructive. They are our associates and helpers in our spiritual struggles and social progress.' A view with which he could not agree, and he marked his dissent by shaking his head. Then referring to the lateness of the hour, he jocularly remarked, 'It is time for you to depart. Take care, do not be late, otherwise your woman will not admit you into her room.' This evoked hearty laughter.

Pratap Chandra Mazumdar, Keshab's right-hand man and an accomplished Brahmo preacher in Europe and America, bitterly criticized Sri Ramakrishna's use of uncultured language and also his austere attitude towards his wife. But at the same time he could not escape the spell of the Master's personality. In the course of an article about Sri Ramakrishna, Pratap wrote in the *Theistic Quarterly Review*:

What is common between him and me? I, Europeanized, civilized, self-centred, semi-sceptical, so-called educated, reasoned, and he a poor, illiterate, unpolished, half-idolatrous, friendless Hindu devotee? Why should I sit long hours to attend to him? I who have listened to Disraeli and Fawcett, Stanley and Max Mueller, and a whole host of European scholars and divines? And it is not Kali only, but he worships Rama, he worships Krishna and is a confirmed advocate of Vedantic doctrines. He is an idolater, yet is a faithful and most devoted meditator on the perfections of the One formless, absolute, infinite deity . . . his religion is ecstasy, his worship means transcendental insight, his whole nature burns day and night with a permanent fire and fever of a strange faith and feeling.

So long as he is available to us, gladly shall we sit at his feet to learn from him the sublime precepts of purity, unworldliness, spirituality and inebriation in the love of God. He, by his childlike bhakti, by his strong conceptions of an ever-ready Motherhood, helped to unfold it (God as our Mother) in our minds wonderfully . . . by associating with him we learnt to realize better the divine attributes as scattered over the three hundred and thirty millions of deities of mythological India, the gods of the Puranas.

The Brahmo Samaj leaders received great inspiration through their contact with Sri Ramakrishna. It broadened their religious views and kindled in their hearts the yearning for God. It made them understand and appreciate the rituals and symbols of the Hindu religion. It also convinced them of the manifestation of God in diverse forms, and deepened their thoughts about the harmony of religions. The Master too, was impressed by the sincerity of many of the Brahmo devotees. He told them about his own realizations and explained the essence of his teachings, such as the necessity of renunciation, sincerity in the pursuit of one's own course of discipline, faith in God, the performance of one's duties without giving any thought to results and discrimination between the real and the unreal.

This contact with the educated and progressive Bengalis opened Sri Ramakrishna's eyes to a new realm of thought. Born and brought up in a simple village, without any formal education and taught by the orthodox holy men of India in religious life, he had had no opportunity to study the influence of modernism on the thoughts and lives of the Hindus. He could not properly estimate the result of the impact of Western education on Indian culture. He was a Hindu of the Hindus, renunciation being the only means to the realization of God in life. From the Brahmos he learnt that the new generation of India made a compromise between God and the world. Educated young men were influenced more by the Western philosophers than by their own prophets. But Sri Ramakrishna was not dismayed, for he saw in this, too, the hand of God. And though he expounded to the Brahmos all his ideas about God and austere religious disciplines, yet he asked them to accept from his teachings only as much as the lessons suited their tastes and temperaments.

Contact with the Brahmos increased Sri Ramakrishna's longing to encounter aspirants who would be able to follow his teachings in their purest form. He once declared:

There was no limit to the longing I felt at that time. During daytime, I somehow managed to control it. The secular talk of the worldly mind was galling to me, and I would look wistfully to the day when my own beloved companions would come. I hoped to find solace in conversing with them and relating to them my own realizations. Every little incident would remind me of them, and thoughts of them engrossed me fully. I was already arranging in my mind what I should say to one and give to another and so on. But when the day came to a close I would not be able to curb my feelings. The thought that another day had gone by, and they had not come, depressed me. When during the course of the evening service, the temples rang with the sound of bells and conch shells, I climbed to the roof of the *kuti* in the garden and, writhing in anguish, say, 'I cannot bear to live without you.' A mother never longed so intensely for the sight of her child, nor a friend for his companions, or a lover for his beloved, as I longed for them. Oh, it was indescribable!

Shortly, after this period of yearning the devotees began to come.

By the year 1879, occasional writings about Sri Ramakrishna began to appear in the Brahmo magazines. Those writings began to attract his future disciples from the educated, middle-class Bengali people, and they continued to come till 1884. But others came too, feeling the subtle power of his attraction. They were an ever-shifting crowd of people of all castes and creeds: Hindus, Brahmos, Vaishnavas, Saktas, the educated with university degrees and the illiterates, old and young, maharajas, beggars, journalists, artists, pandits, devotees, the innocent and the worldly minded, yogis, men of action and men of faith, virtuous women, even prostitutes, office holders, vagabonds, philanthropists, self-seekers, dramatists, drunkards, builders. People came from all walks of life. He gave to them all, without stint, from his infinite store of realization. No one left empty-handed. He taught them the lofty knowledge of the Vedanta and the soul-melting love of the Puranas. Twenty hours out of twenty-four he would speak without rest or respite. He gave to all his sympathy and enlightenment, and he touched them with that strange power of the soul, which could not but melt even the most hardened souls. People understood him according to their own powers of comprehension.

His disciples were of two kinds: the householders, and the young men, some of whom went on to become monks later. There was also a small group of women devotees.

To those who were householders, he did not prescribe the difficult path of total renunciation. He wanted them to discharge their obligations to their families. Their renunciation was to be mental. Spiritual life could not be acquired by running away from responsibilities. A married couple should live like brother and sister after the birth of one or two children, devoting their time to spiritual talk and contemplation. He encouraged the householders by saying that their life was, in a way, easier than that of the monks, since it was more advantageous to fight the enemy from inside a fortress than in an open field. However, he insisted on their going into solitude periodically to strengthen their devotion and faith in God, through prayer and meditation. He urged them to stay in the company of sadhus. In addition, he advised them to perform their worldly duties as early as they could, so that they became free of their duties and responsibilities towards their family members and were able to cling to Him with both hands in the end. He would discourage, in both the householders and the celibate youths, any lukewarm or light attitude towards their spiritual struggles. He never asked them to follow the ideal of non-resistance indiscriminately, for he believed that it ultimately makes a coward of the unwary.

But to the young men destined to be monks, he pointed out the steep path of renunciation, both external and internal. They had to take a vow of absolute continence and eschew all thoughts of greed and lust. By practising continence, aspirants developed a subtle nerve through which they attained a deeper understanding of the mysteries of God. For them self-control was the final imperative and absolute. The sannyasis are teachers of men and their lives should be totally blemish-free. They were not allowed to even look at a picture which might awaken their animal passions. The Master selected his future monks from young men untouched by 'women and gold' and who were malleable enough to be cast in his spiritual mould. While teaching them the path of renunciation and discrimination, he never allowed the householders to be anywhere in the vicinity.

Of the first two householder devotees to come to Dakshineswar, Ramachandra Dutta and Manmohan Mitra, it was Ram who introduced Narendranath, his relative, to Sri Ramakrishna.

The first of the young men to come to the Master was Latu. Born to poor parents in Bihar, he came to Calcutta in search of work and was engaged by Ramachandra Dutta as a houseboy. Latu was so taken with the personality of the Master on his visits to Dakshineswar that he asked Ramachandra if he might serve Sri Ramakrishna for the rest of his life. An illiterate, orphaned, country boy from an impoverished area, rough-hewn Latu showed an amazing aptitude for spirituality. When Latu took his vows and was rechristened Swami Adbhutananda, 'God,' Sri Ramakrishna said affectionately, 'had passed a camel through the eye of a needle.'

One day a young, lean, seventeen-year-old boy arrived at the door of Dakshineswar with Manmohan Mitra. Ramakrishna smiled with recognition and called him in. He made him sit next to him and with great affection stroked his head and gazed at his face. With immense delight he said, 'I asked Mother Kali for a boy just as I was, pure hearted and intensely devoted to Her, to be my constant companion. She showed you to me in a dream. And now it has come true.' Rakhal smiled and asked, 'Do you truly know God? I yearn for him unceasingly.'

Rakhal, whom Ramakrishna called his *manasaputra*, his mind-born son, came from a wealthy landowning family. He arrived at Dakshineswar with the intention of serving Sri Ramakrishna, but his capacity for devotion was such, his absorption with the inner light so great, it rendered him incapable of normal work. Sri Ramakrishna looked after Rakhal and took care of him. Later, he went on to become Swami Brahmananda, the first abbot of the Ramakrishna Mission.

Even before Rakhal's arrival at Dakshineswar, the Master had visions of him as his spiritual son and as a playmate of Krishna at Vrindavan. During his childhood, Rakhal developed wonderful spiritual traits and played at worshipping gods and goddesses. In his teens he was married to Manmohan Mitra's sister. He heard about the Master from Manmohan. His father objected to his association with Sri Ramakrishna, but was later reassured to find that many celebrated people were visitors at Dakshineswar. The relationship between the Master and this beloved disciple resembled that of mother and child. Sri Ramakrishna allowed him many liberties denied to other boys. Rakhal soon realized that his guru was the Guru of the entire universe. The Master was worried to hear of his marriage, but was relieved to find that his wife was a spiritual soul who would not be a hindrance to his progress.

One day the young, impetuous Rakhal impatient for his first samadhi, stormed out of Dakshineswar in frustration and was stopped mysteriously at the gate by an unknown force, till he learned to submit.

Gopal Ghosh was the oldest of the newcomers, a paper merchant, grieving over the loss of his wife, looking to religion for answers to life's sufferings. After taking the sannyasa vows he was to become Swami Advitananda. But it was not as though his disciples fell into line, losing their human foibles overnight. Nor, even, that Sri Ramakrishna was unable to see the flaws in every character, or to overlook those that he did see. With the clarity of his inner eye, he saw deep into each man's soul, and gently, without confrontation, more subtly than any modern psychotherapist, he steered him along the path that led out of the thickets and jungles of emotional convolution to the empowering plains of ability and the clear high mountains of the spirit.

And so they came as Sri Ramakrishna's fame spread. His spiritual sons formed the nucleus of the Ramakrishna Order – formalized as the Ramakrishna Mission in 1897 – and Sarada Devi was the Mother after the death of the mortal frame of Sri Ramakrishna. They carried the experiences of the humble village priest forward to the next century.

Many new faces were now seen in Dakshineswar, but it soon became evident that it was time for one old face to leave. Good, capable, competent, loyal Hriday was unable to resist the power that accrued to him as the closest and longest lasting attendant to a sage whose following was growing in geometric progression every day. He bullied priests and temple staff, even Sri Ramakrishna himself. Eventually, Hriday was persuaded to leave the premises of the temple, forever.

Sri Ramakrishna could not have asked for more devotees or more disciples. But yet to come was Narendranath Datta, the gifted, brilliant, flamboyant, highly educated son of a wealthy and aristocratic family, who became Sri Ramakrishna's greatest miracle – Swami Vivekananda – to carry his vision not just across the land, but across the seas, to make it a truly universal creed.

Naren was someone Sri Ramakrishna begged the Divine Mother to send him, someone who would question his realizations. It was a prayer that Naren was to fulfil in abundance.

Six

Taming the Bull

O my mind let us go home – Why do you roam
The earth, that foreign land
And wear its alien garb?
These senses, these elements
Are strangers; none is your own . . .
Why do you forget yourself
Falling in love with strangers?
O my mind, why do you
Forget your own?

Sri Ramakrishna and his group

$\mathscr{S}$ri Ramakrishna began to mould his torchbearers who later crystallized and embodied his insights and teachings, going out into the materialistic world and bringing to it a special brand of activism bred of deep spiritual insights. He yearned for a spiritual heir who would challenge and question his realizations, who would be fired with that special zeal. Before his true disciples arrived and before he trained them to spread his mission far and wide, Ramakrishna himself encountered people with different viewpoints, who too believed in serving the ailing humanity, but had different methods of doing so. Ramakrishna had a unique method and approach which was more sustainable in the long run.

Through his life, Ramakrishna came into contact with a number of people whose scholarship or wealth brought them respect everywhere they went. But few had the divine spark that he searched for. When he met Devendranath Tagore, famous all over Bengal for his wealth, scholarship, saintly character and social position, he was disappointed, for Sri Ramakrishna had expected to meet a saint who had completely renounced the world. Instead, he found that Devendranath combined his saintliness with a life of enjoyment. He also met the great poet, Michael Madhusudan, who had embraced Christianity 'for the sake of his stomach'. To him, the Master could not impart any instruction, for the Divine Mother 'pressed his tongue' when he tried to do so. In addition, he met Maharaja Jatindra Mohan Tagore, a titled aristocrat of Bengal; Kristodas Pal, editor, social reformer and a patriot; Iswar Chandra Vidyasagar, the noted philanthropist and educator; Pandit Shashadhar, a great champion of Hindu orthodoxy; Aswini Kumar Dutta, a headmaster, moralist and a leader of Indian nationalism; and Bankim Chandra Chatterji, a deputy magistrate, novelist and essayist. A pandit without discrimination, he regarded them as mere straws. He searched people's hearts for the light of God and if that was missing he did not have anything further to do with them.

The Europeanized Kristodas Pal did not approve of the Master's emphasis on renunciation and said: 'Sir, this concept of renunciation has almost ruined the country. It is for this reason that the Indians are a subject nation today. Doing good to others, bringing education to the door of the ignorant and, above all, improving the material conditions of the country – these should be our duty now. Religion and renunciation would, on the contrary, only weaken us. You should advise the young men of Bengal to resort only to such acts as will uplift the country.'

Sri Ramakrishna gave him a searching look and found no divine light within him.

You dare to slight renunciation and piety in these terms, when our scriptures describe them as the greatest of all virtues! After reading two pages of English you think you know the world! You appear to think you are omniscient. Well, have you seen those tiny crabs that are born in the Ganga just when the rains set in? In this big universe, you are even less significant than one of those small creatures. How dare you talk of helping the world? The Lord will look to that. You haven't the power in you to do it.

After a pause the Master continued:

Can you explain to me how you can work for others? I know what you mean by helping them. To feed a number of people, to treat them when they are sick, to construct a road or dig a well – isn't that all? These are good deeds, no doubt, but how trifling compared with the vastness of the universe! How far can a man advance along this line? How many people can you save from famine? Malaria has ruined a whole province; what could you do to stop its onslaught? God alone looks after the world. Let a man first realize Him. Let a man get the authority from God and be endowed with His power; then, and then alone, may he think of doing good to others. A man should first be purged of all egotism. Then alone will the blissful Mother ask him to work for the world.

Sri Ramakrishna mistrusted philanthropy that presumed to pose as charity. He warned people against it. He saw in most acts of philanthropy nothing but egotism, vanity, a desire for glory, a barren excitement to kill the boredom of life, or an attempt to soothe a guilty conscience. True charity, he taught, is the result of love of God – service to man in a spirit of worship.

The day the Master met Narendranath Datta was the most cataclysmic moment in the lives of Sri Ramakrishna and Naren, as he was lovingly called. This meeting did not promise smooth sailing for either. Both had to tread a difficult path together and individually, in accepting each other. If it was not for the Master's unconditional love for Naren and the direction that he constantly got from the Divine Mother, it would not have been the great Master–student relationship as Ramakrishna and Vivekananda that the world knows today.

When the Master first saw Naren, he was singing a bhajan in a deep haunting voice. The guests assembled were from the upper strata of society and Naren was dressed carelessly with

Swami Vivekananda

his hair tousled, but he was in a deep state of concentration. Sri Ramakrishna was deeply moved by the singing and nodded his head in approval.

It was not that Naren had not heard of Sri Ramakrishna; he simply was not interested in him. The principal of Naren's college, W.W. Hastie, one of the few Englishmen who had a profound understanding of India's culture, had urged Naren to go to Dakshineswar. 'To understand the nature-mysticism of Wordsworth,' he said 'you must understand states of deep meditation, such as that I have witnessed Sri Ramakrishna experience.'

To spread his message to the four corners of the earth, Sri Ramakrishna needed a strong instrument. With his frail body and delicate limbs, he knew that he could not make great journeys across wide spaces. And he found such an instrument in his beloved Naren, who was later known to the world as Swami Vivekananda. Even before meeting Naren, the Master had seen him in his visions when he was immersed in the meditation of the Absolute. He saw him in the form of a sage, who at Sri Ramakrishna's request, agreed to take human birth to assist him in his work.

Narendranath was born in Calcutta on 12 January 1863, of an aristocratic Kayastha family. His mother was steeped in the great Hindu epics and his father, a distinguished attorney of the Calcutta High Court, was agnostic about religion, a friend of the poor, and a mocker of social conventions. Even in his boyhood and teens, Narendra possessed great physical courage and presence of mind, a vivid imagination, deep power of thought, keen intelligence, an extraordinary memory, love of truth, passion for purity, spirit of independence and, above all, a tender heart. An expert musician, he also acquired proficiency in physics, astronomy, mathematics, philosophy, history and literature. He grew up to be an extremely handsome young man. Even as a child, he practised meditation and showed great powers of concentration. Though free and passionate in word and action, he took the vow of austere religious chastity and never allowed the fire of purity to be extinguished by the slightest defilement of body or soul.

As his college studies progressed, the rationalistic Western philosophers of the nineteenth century unsettled his boyhood faith in God and religion. He never accepted religion on mere 'faith'. He wanted some kind of demonstration of God. But very soon his passionate nature discovered that mere universal reason was cold and bloodless. His emotional nature, dissatisfied with a mere abstraction, required concrete support to help him in times of temptation. He wanted an external power, a guru, who by embodying perfection in the flesh would still the commotion of his soul. Attracted by Keshab's magnetic personality, he joined the Brahmo Samaj and became a singer in its choir. But within the Samaj, he did not come across a single person or find the guru whom he was desperately seeking, who could say that he had seen God.

During the first meeting of Ramakrishna and Naren, Ramakrishna was immensely impressed and looked at his face intently. Naren was uncomfortable and embarrassed by this close scrutiny. Sri Ramakrishna questioned him, but Naren answered in a distant manner.

Talented, sporty, energetic, restless, aggressively independent, disciplined – Narendranath was a natural leader, unconventional in outlook, careless of social sanction, and with an iron will. At eighteen, struggling with the nature of creation and death and the presence of evil, he challenged the existence of God and found himself heading in the only direction that pure reason untempered by intuition could take him – towards agnosticism.

One day Ramachandra Dutta, who was related to Naren, told him, 'I hear you turned down that marriage proposal again. Your parents are terrified you're going to remain celibate and become a sadhu like your grandfather.' Naren replied, 'When I was a child, I thought sadhus were the very embodiment of heroic freedom, they were giants forging their own way through the world, heedless of the views of society, slaves to no man.' The curious Ramachandra Dutta asked, 'And now?' Naren shrugged wryly and replied, 'I wonder – does the Divine not come out of the creative imagination of man's long childhood?' Ramachandra Dutta unbelievingly said, 'Uh huh! You won't find spiritual life at the Brahmo Samaj, Naren. You must accept Sri Ramakrishna's invitation. I'll take you to Dakshineswar myself.'

'After my exams,' Naren replied, as he did not like being pressured. Ramachandra Dutta acknowledged the evasion and agreed.

It was not that Naren had not searched for God. He yearned for a faith he could embrace with his whole being, a faith stretching far beyond the narrow circle of reason, a faith wide enough to encompass the universe. Once, while listening to Devendranath Tagore speaking eloquently of God, Naren asked him point-blank, 'But Sir, have you *seen* Him?' The erudite leader of the Brahmo Samaj had not, and none of those who preached of God had either. Preachers cited earlier preachers, who cited earlier preachers. And their sermons were collections of lifeless quotations out of books; nothing they said seemed to come out of lived experience.

'If God actually exists,' Naren reasoned, 'there must be irrefutable evidence. Somewhere there must be those who put Him to the test and proved Him in the laboratories of their own experience as plainly and as unsentimentally as Western scientists proved the laws of nature.' Four days after Naren met Sri Ramakrishna at Surendranath Mitra's residence, he arrived at Dakshineswar with Ramachandra Dutta. When they got there, Ramakrishna was in his room with a group of devotees, meditating. Sri Ramakrishna was told about the arrival of the new guests. He opened his eyes, showed great delight and gestured Naren to sit on the mat. He asked, 'Do you know any Bengali songs? You sing so well.' Naren began to sing.

O my mind let us go home – Why do you roam
The earth, that foreign land
And wear its alien garb?
These senses, these elements
Are strangers; none is your own . . .
Why do you forget yourself
Falling in love with strangers?
O my mind, why do you
Forget your own?

On hearing the song, Ramakrishna went into samadhi. Naren was startled and felt uneasy. To add to his discomfiture, Ramakrishna grabbed him by his hand, drew him out to the veranda and wept, saying, 'What took you so long? Could you not have guessed how much I've been waiting for you? My ears are burned off listening to the talk of these worldly people! I thought I should burst not having anyone to tell how I really felt.'

Naren was astonished beyond words and could hardly get over the initial shock when Ramakrishna continued, 'I know you, my lord. You are the Rishi Nara, the incarnation of Narayana. You've come to remove the miseries and sufferings of humanity.' Naren, who continued to be stunned, held himself back and suddenly Ramakrishna said, 'Wait a moment.' He went into the room, returned with a dish of sweets and fed Naren. He fed him mouthful after mouthful and said, 'Promise me you will come again . . . alone.'

Naren was doubtful, but Ramakrishna was earnest. Naren was polite yet hesitant to promise, but against his will said, 'Yes . . . all right, I will.' Delighted and relieved as a child,

Ramakrishna then took Naren back to the room and spoke to the devotees with great inspiration, 'God can be seen and spoken to just as I am speaking to you. But who wants to speak to God? People grieve and shed enough tears to fill many pots because their wives or sons are dead, or because they've lost their money and estates. But who weeps because he hasn't seen God?'

Naren listened to the Master's words and suddenly, with great intensity, asked, 'Sir, have *you* seen God?' And Ramakrishna spontaneously replied, 'I have seen Him just as I see you. I have spoken to Him as I am speaking to you. If a man truly desires to see God and calls upon Him with a longing heart, He surely reveals himself.'

'Is it the same man?' Naren thought looking at Sri Ramakrishna who seemed normal again after that bizarre scene in the veranda. 'He's not like all those other preachers full of poetic bombast . . . Well, he may be a monomaniac, but it is a great soul who can undertake such renunciation. Yes, he *is* mad. But how pure! And what renunciation!'

Naren went up to Sri Ramakrishna and touched his feet and took leave of him. Sri Ramakrishna was left with a longing for him to come back. But Naren did not return for a month. The meeting with Sri Ramakrishna disturbed him violently – as it had Keshab Chandra Sen and Ramachandra Dutta. But more than others Naren feared Sri Ramakrishna's possible influence over himself.

Although he was dissatisfied with the spiritual life of the Brahmo Samaj, he was enthusiastic about its reformist ideals. He was critical of the traditional Hinduism for which Sri Ramakrishna stood. He believed in reason rather than intuition, in discrimination rather than devotion.

As Naren walked back to Calcutta he told himself that Sri Ramakrishna was crazy. Yet, in spite of himself he felt almost ready to follow him. But no! How could he become a disciple to a mad man? Sri Ramakrishna *must* be mad.

Sri Ramakrishna eluded judgement. He did not fit ordinary categories. He was a challenge and a riddle in every sense. His devotion challenged Naren's sense of propriety, his serenity challenged Naren's restlessness. Despite his reservations towards him, Naren was drawn to Sri Ramakrishna and he went back to Dakshineswar. When he arrived the Master was meditating in his room. Naren sat in front of him. The Master opened his eyes and looked at Naren neutrally, muttered something and put his foot on him. Naren felt the whole room whirling and he cried out, 'What are you doing to me? Don't you know I have parents at home?' Ramakrishna removed his foot and said, 'All right, let it stop now. It need not all be done at once. It will happen in its own good time.' Naren struggled with this experience as he had with the first. Had he been hypnotized? But he prided himself on his strong mind. Besides, the experience he had when Sri Ramakrishna touched him was hardly that of a hypnotic stupor. He decided to be on guard the next time.

But the next time Sri Ramakrishna touched Naren, he fell unconscious instantly. Sri Ramakrishna said, later, that during this time he questioned Naren closely on his past lives and ascertained that he was indeed the reincarnation of the sage Nara. But all that Naren was convinced of was that he was in the presence of a being with a far greater will than his own. To that he *would* not submit; it was *wrong* to surrender his freedom of judgement to another.

Had Sri Ramakrishna not been, at the same time, a trusting, open and naive child, undoubtedly Naren would never have returned a third time, for there is nothing more repugnant than being manipulated by a hard, adult personality who is stronger than you. Yet Naren returned again and again. He had decided he would test Sri Ramakrishna at every stage.

The violence of Naren's struggle against his Master made him the most reliable witness to Sri Ramakrishna's greatness. 'Let none regret,' Naren said later to hesitant disciples, 'that they were difficult to convince. I fought my Master for six long years, with the result that I now know every inch of the way.'

One day, Naren was walking with Rakhal in the temple courtyard towards the Kali temple when he sarcastically said, 'The Master's had me reading texts on *advaita*. Rakhal, this non-dualism is nonsense. "I'm God you're God, everything that is born and dies is God!" The authors of these books must have been mad. How can a created soul think of itself as the creator? *Advaita* muddles everything together in a formless, tasteless, cosmic soup.'

Rakhal smiled tolerantly and moved off to the temple and Naren asked, 'Where are you going?' Rakhal teasingly replied, 'To worship Kali. Most dualistically. You should approve.' This irritated Naren and he said, 'Now you're going to prostrate yourself before a hunk of stone! For heaven's sake, Rakhal, where are your brains?'

The philosophic dialectic of the West is analytical. The intellect struggles to make sharp distinctions between things, to untangle knotted strands and trace pathways, to make order out of the seeming chaos of the universe. It works by dividing and conquering, by breaking up the universe into logically manageable chunks and manipulating them to the dictates of the intellect. The price paid for this way of thinking (as we have seen to our cost) is that we forget that things are whole to begin with. We see ourselves and objects and events as loosely bound independent units, whose fundamental truth consists in separateness and not in unity with the cosmos.

One day, as Naren sat with the group of devotees in the courtyard, he said sarcastically, 'Can it be that this water pot is God? Or this jug? Is it God? And everything we see is God? And *you* are God?' Some devotees laughed genuinely and some hesitatingly when Sri Ramakrishna asked, 'What are you laughing about?' He gently touched Naren's shoulder. Suddenly, Naren saw with wonder, light emanating from the jug and water pot. It was the same light that emanated from the jug that also emanated from the water pot and it blinded Naren. The same light surrounded the temple courtyard, trees and everywhere that Naren looked.

Words were Naren's native element. He swam in conceptualization as a fish in water. He used his intellect as a sharp blade to cleave the true from the false. Sri Ramakrishna said, 'Knowledge can get you to God's living room. But it is love that will take you into his inner apartment.' Refusing to battle Naren on his terms with endless argument, Sri Ramakrishna showed him, wordlessly, with a touch, the reality of *advaita*.

This was Naren who was to become Swami Vivekananda, Sri Ramakrishna's foremost disciple, his mouthpiece to the world. It was not for nothing that Romain Rolland said years later that Sri Ramakrishna and Vivekananda displayed together 'the splendid symphony of the universal soul'.

As Naren's training continued over the years, other disciples came to Sri Ramakrishna and eventually became part of his inner circle. Six of them Sri Ramakrishna called Ishwarkotis, beings who had always been liberated from the enjoyments of worldly objects, therefore, free from the bondage of the results of karma, but had allowed themselves to be born to serve mankind and live in a loving relation with God. Foremost amongst Sri Ramakrishna's Ishwarkotis were Naren and Rakhal.

Seven

Disciples

If bricks and tiles
are burnt after the trademark
has been stamped on them,
they retain the mark forever.

Disciples:

(1) Mahendra or M. (3) Kali (5) Sarat (6) Mani Mallick (7) Gangadhar (8) Navagopal (11) Tarak (13) the elder Gopal (15) Vaikuntha (17) Manmohan (18) Harish (19) Narayan (21) Shashi (22) Latu (23) Bhavanath (24) Baburam (25) Niranjan (26) Narendra (27) Ramchandra Dutta (28) Balaram Bose (29) Rakhal (30) Nityagopal (31) Jogindra (32) Debendranath Mazumdar

*B*aburam Ghosh, who was to become Swami Premananda, came to Dakshineswar accompanied by his classmate Rakhal. The Master, as was often his custom, examined the boy's physiognomy and was satisfied about his latent spirituality. At the age of eight, Baburam had thought of leading a life of renunciation in the company of a monk, in a hut shut away from public view by a thick wall of trees. The very sight of Panchavati awakened in his heart that boyhood dream. Baburam was tender in body and soul. The Master would say that he was pure to his very bones. One day, Hazra – who was one of the devotees – in his usual mischievous fashion advised Baburam and some of the other young boys to ask Sri Ramakrishna for some spiritual powers and not waste their life in mere gaiety and merriment. The Master, scenting mischief, called Baburam to his side and said, 'What can you ask of me? Isn't everything that I have already yours? Yes, everything I have earned in the shape of realizations is for all of you. So, get rid of the idea of begging, which alienates an individual by creating a distance. Rather, realize your kinship with me and gain the key to all the treasures.'

Nityaniranjan Ghosh, who was to become Swami Niranjanananda, had established clairvoyant powers before he came to Dakshineswar. Powers he soon discarded. He was especially devoted to Sarada Ma after Sri Ramakrishna's death.

Niranjan was a heroic disciple. He came to the Master when he was eighteen, a mediocre achiever in a group of spiritualists – those who engaged in the realm of netherworld spirits. The Master told him during his first visit, 'My boy, if you think always of ghosts you will become a ghost, and if you think of God you will become God. Now, which do you prefer?' Niranjan severed all connections with the spiritualists. During his second visit, the Master embraced him and said warmly, 'Niranjan, the days are flitting away. When will you realize God? This life will be in vain if you do not realize Him. When will you devote your mind wholly to God?' Niranjan was surprised to see the Master's great anxiety for his spiritual development. He felt disdain for worldly pleasures and was totally guileless like a child. Yet he had a violent temper. One day, as he was coming in a country boat to Dakshineswar, some of his fellow passengers began to speak ill of the Master. Finding his protests futile, Niranjan began to rock the boat and threatened to sink it in midstream. That silenced the offenders. When he reported the incident to the Master, he was rebuked for his inability to curb his anger.

Yogindranath Raychaudhury, on the other hand, was gentle to a fault. One day, under circumstances very similar to those that had evoked Niranjan's anger, he curbed his temper and held his peace, instead of threatening Sri Ramakrishna's abusers. The Master learned of his conduct too and scolded him soundly. Thus, to each, the fault of the other was recommended as a virtue. The guru attempted to develop, in the first instance, composure, and in the second, mettle. The secret of his training was to build up the distinctive character of a devotee, by tactful recognition of the requirements of each disciple.

Yogindranath came from an aristocratic Brahmin family of Dakshineswar. His father and relatives shared the popular mistrust of Sri Ramakrishna's sanity. From a very tender age the boy developed religious tendencies. He spent two to three hours daily in meditation and his meeting with Sri Ramakrishna deepened his desire for the realization of God. He was horrified by the thought of marriage. But at the earnest request of his mother he had to give in and, thereafter, he believed that his spiritual future was doomed. So he kept himself away from the Master.

Sri Ramakrishna employed a ruse to bring Yogindranath to him. As soon as the disciple entered the room the Master rushed forward to meet the young man. He caught hold of the disciple's hand and said, 'What if you have got married? Haven't I too been married all this while? What is there to be afraid of in that?' Touching his own chest, he said, 'If this is propitious, then even a hundred thousand marriages cannot injure you. If you desire to lead a householder's life, then bring your wife here one day. But if you wish to lead a monastic life, then I shall eat up your attachment to the world.' Yogin was dumbfounded. He received new strength and his spirit of renunciation was re-established.

Yogindranath, who was to become Swami Yogananda, had at first visited Sri Ramakrishna secretly, because his family disapproved of the madman of Dakshineswar. Till Sri Ramakrishna passed away, Yogananda, while loving Vivekananda dearly, was often at loggerheads with him over his liberal attitudes. He too, served Sarada Devi closely until his death.

The sixth was Purna Chandra Ghosh. Purna came surreptitiously to Dakshineswar when he was thirteen because his family, too, disapproved of Sri Ramakrishna. He could not take sannyas, however, as family circumstances forced him to marry – but he was close to the Ramakrishna Order and revered for his spiritual greatness. Sri Ramakrishna described Purna as an Ishwarkoti, a soul born with special spiritual qualities. The Master said that Purna was the last of the group of brilliant devotees who, as he once had seen in a trance, would come to him for spiritual illumination. Purna told the Master during their second meeting, 'You are God Himself, incarnated in flesh and blood.' Such words coming from a mere youngster showed his rich spirituality and also proved what strong stuff the boy was made up of.

Others, Sri Ramakrishna termed nityasiddhas, the ever-perfect. Destined to be monastic disciples of Sri Ramakrishna, they all came to Dakshineswar.

Saratchandra Chakrabarty was only eighteen when he arrived at Sri Ramakrishna's doorstep. He gave up his medical studies to look after Sri Ramakrishna when he became fatally ill and never returned to that world. He later became the monk Swami Saradananda, took charge of Vivekananda's Bengali magazine, *Udbodhan* or *Awakening*, and wrote Sri Ramakrishna's biography.

Sashi and Sarat were two cousins who came from a pious Brahmin family of Calcutta. At a very early age they joined the Brahmo Samaj and came under the influence of Keshab Sen. The Master told them at their first meeting:

> If bricks and tiles are burnt after the trademark has been stamped on them, they retain the mark forever. Similarly, man should be stamped with God before entering the world. Then he will not become attached to worldliness.

Fully aware of the future course of their lives he asked them not to marry. The Master asked Sashi whether he believed in God who had a form or one without form. Sashi replied that he was not even sure about the existence of God, so he could not comment one way or the other. This frank answer pleased the Master very much.

Sarat's soul longed for the all-embracing realization of God. When the Master enquired whether there was any particular form of God he wished to see, the boy replied that he would like to see God in all the living beings of the world. 'But,' the Master demurred, 'that is the last word in realization. One cannot have it at the very outset.' Sarat replied calmly, 'I won't be satisfied with anything short of that. I shall trudge on along the path till I attain that blessed state.' Sri Ramakrishna was very pleased.

Sashibhusan Chakravarty, Sarat's cousin, would become Swami Ramakrishnananda, a great devotee. He had a brilliant intellect and was especially fond of astronomy and mathematics. He founded the first branch of the Ramakrishna Mission in Madras.

Taraknath Ghosal's father had been legal adviser to Rani Rasmani, so Tarak was not unaware of Sri Ramakrishna as a child. Tarak had felt from his boyhood the noble desire to realize God. Keshab and the Brahmo Samaj attracted him but proved inadequate. In 1882 he first met the Master at Ramachandra's house and was astonished to hear him talk about samadhi, a subject that always fascinated his mind. That evening he actually saw a manifestation of that super-conscious state in the Master. Tarak, whose marriage did not come in the way of his devotion, became a frequent visitor at Dakshineswar and received the Master's grace in abundance. The young boy often felt ecstatic fervours in meditation. He also wept profusely while meditating. To him, Sri Ramakrishna said, 'God favours those who can weep for Him. Tears shed for God wash away the sins of former births.'

Like many young Brahmos, he began to understand the value of Sri Ramakrishna's teachings later in life. He became Swami Shivananda, and after Sri Ramakrishna's death spent years as a wandering monk, before becoming the second President of the Ramakrishna Order after the death of Swami Brahmananda.

Harinath Chatterjee, who was to become Swami Turiyananda, was drawn to the meditative, ascetic life as a child. He first saw Sri Ramakrishna in samadhi at the home of Surendranath Mitra when he was fourteen and came to Dakshineswar four years later. He reluctantly joined Naren, Swami Vivekananda, on his second tour of the US and found himself initiating and running the Shanti Ashram in San Antonio Valley in California, for two years. Harinath had led the austere life of a *brahmachari* even from his early boyhood – waking before sunrise, reciting the Gita from memory before leaving his bed in the morning, bathing in the Ganga every day and cooking his own meals. He found in the Master the embodiment of the Vedanta scriptures. Aspiring to be a follower of the ascetic Sankar, he cherished a great hatred for women. One day he said that he could not allow even little girls to come near him. The Master scolded him and said, 'You are talking like a fool. Why should you hate women? They are the manifestations of the Divine Mother. Regard them as your own mother and you will never feel their evil influence. The more you hate them, the more you will fall into their snares.'

Hari admitted later that these words completely changed his attitude towards women.

The Master knew Hari's passion for Vedanta. But he did not wish any of his disciples to become dry ascetics or mere bookworms. Therefore, he asked Hari to practise Vedanta in life by giving up the unreal and following the real. 'But it is not so easy,' Sri Ramakrishna said, 'to realize the illusoriness of the world. Study alone does not help one very much. The grace of God is required. Mere personal effort is futile. A man is a tiny creature after all, with very limited powers. But he can achieve the impossible if he prays to God for His grace.'

Then the Master sang a song in praise of grace. Hari was moved to tears. Later in life, Hari achieved a wonderful synthesis of the ideals of the personal God and impersonal truth.

Durgacharan Nag was a homeopathic physician from East Bengal, who was so influenced by Sri Ramakrishna's teachings that he became known throughout Bengal as a saint in his own right, for the humility and devotion with which he regarded the humblest of his fellow men. Durgacharan, also known as Nag Mahashay, was the ideal householder among the lay disciples of Sri Ramakrishna. He was an embodiment of the Master's ideal of life, unstained by worldliness. In spite of his intense desire to become a sannyasi, Sri Ramakrishna asked him to live in the world in the spirit of a monk, and the disciple truly carried out his injunction. He was born of a poor family and even during his boyhood often sacrificed everything to lessen the sufferings of the needy and downtrodden. He married at an early age and after his wife's death married a second time to obey his father's command. But he once said to his wife, 'Love on the physical level never lasts. He is indeed blessed who can give his love to God with his whole heart. Even a little attachment to the body endures for several births. So, do not be attached to this cage of bone and flesh. Take shelter at the feet of the Mother and think of Her alone. Thus your life here and hereafter will be ennobled.'

The Master compared him to a 'blazing light'. He received every word of Sri Ramakrishna in dead earnest. One day he heard the Master saying that it was difficult for doctors, lawyers and brokers to make much progress in spirituality. Of doctors he said, 'If the mind clings to the tiny drops of medicine, how can it conceive the infinite?' That was the end of Durgacharan's medical practice and he knew that he would not lack simple food and clothing. Ramakrishna asked him to serve holy men. On being asked where he would find real holy men, the Master said that the sadhus themselves would seek his company. No sannyasi could have lived a more austere life than Durgacharan.

Two more young men, Saradaprasanna and Tulasi, completed the small band of the Master's disciples. They embraced the life of the wandering monk later in life. With the exception of the older Gopal, all of them were in their teens or slightly over that age. Most of them pursued their studies in either school or college and came from middle-class Bengali families. Though their parents and relatives envisaged bright worldly careers for them, they came to Sri Ramakrishna with pure bodies, vigorous minds and uncontaminated souls. All were born with unusual spiritual attributes. Sri Ramakrishna accepted them, even at first sight, as his children, relatives, friends and companions. His magic touch unfolded their latent spirituality. Later, each according to his measure reflected the life of the Master, becoming a torchbearer of his message across land and sea.

Subodh visited the Master in 1885. At the very first meeting, Sri Ramakrishna said, 'You will succeed. Mother says so. Those whom she sends here will certainly attain spirituality.' During the second meeting the Master wrote something on Subodh's tongue, stroked his body from the navel to the throat and said, 'Awake, Mother! Awake.' He asked the boy to meditate. At once Subodh's latent spirituality was awakened. He felt a current rushing along the spinal column to the brain. Utter joy and bliss filled his soul.

Gangadhar, Harinath's friend, also led a celibate life, that of a strict *brahmachari*, eating vegetarian food cooked with his own hands and devoting himself to the study of the scriptures. He met the Master in 1884 and soon became a member of his inner circle. The Master praised his ascetic habit and attributed it to the spiritual disciplines of his past life. Gangadhar became a close companion of Narendra.

Hariprasanna, a college student, visited the Master in the company of his friends Sashi and Sarat. Sri Ramakrishna showed him great favour by initiating him to spiritual life. As long as he lived, Hariprasanna remembered and observed his Master's advice, 'Even if a woman is pure as gold and rolls on the ground for love of God, it is dangerous for a monk just to look at her.'

Kaliprasad visited the Master towards the end of 1883. He used to meditate deeply and spend his time in the study of the scriptures. Kali was particularly interested in yoga. Feeling the need of a guru in spiritual life, he came to the Master and was promptly accepted as a disciple. The young boy possessed a rational mind and often felt sceptical about the concept of a personal God. The Master said to him, 'Your doubts will soon disappear. Others, too, have passed through such a state of mind. Look at Naren, he now weeps whenever Radha's and Krishna's names are uttered in his presence.' Kali began to see visions of gods and goddesses. Very soon these disappeared and he experienced vastness, infinity, and the other attributes of the impersonal Brahman whenever he was in deep meditation.

Women Disciples

With his women devotees, Sri Ramakrishna established a very sweet relationship. He himself embodied the tender traits of a woman. He dwelt on the highest plane of truth where there was not even the slightest trace of sex, and his innate purity evoked only the noblest emotion in men and women alike. His women devotees often said, 'We seldom looked on Sri Ramakrishna as a member of the male sex. We regarded him as one of us. We never felt any constraints before him. He was our best confidant.' They loved him as their child, friend and teacher. In spiritual discipline he advised them to renounce lust and greed and especially warned them not to fall into men's snares.

Sri Sarada Devi (1852–1920), also called Holy Mother, was the spiritual consort of Sri Ramakrishna. Because of her long and close association with the Master, her reminiscences are especially valuable. After his passing away she continued the spiritual ministry which Sri Ramakrishna had started.

Unsurpassed among the women devotees of the Master, in the richness of her devotion and spiritual experiences was Aghoremani Devi, an orthodox Brahmin woman. Widowed at an early age, she dedicated herself completely to spiritual pursuits. Gopala, the Baby Krishna, was her deity, whom she worshipped following the *vatsalya* attitude of the Vaishnava religion. She regarded Him as her own child. Through Him she satisfied her unassuaged maternal love – cooking for Him, feeding Him, bathing Him, and putting Him to bed. This sweet intimacy with Gopala won her the sobriquet of Gopal Ma or Gopala's mother. For forty years she had lived on the banks of the Ganga in a small, bare room, her only companions being a threadbare copy of the Ramayana and a bag containing her rosary. At the age of sixty, in 1884, she visited Sri Ramakrishna at Dakshineswar. During the second visit, as soon as the Master saw her, he said, 'Oh, you have come! Give me something to eat.' With great hesitation, she gave him some ordinary sweets that she had purchased for him on the way. The Master ate them with relish and asked her to bring him simple curries or sweets prepared with her own hands. Gopal Ma thought him to be a strange kind of monk, for instead of talking of God he always asked for food. She did not want to visit him again, but an irresistible attraction brought her back to the temple garden. She carried with her some simple curries that she had cooked herself.

One early morning at three o'clock, about a year later, Gopal Ma was about to finish her daily devotions, when she was startled to find Sri Ramakrishna sitting on her left, with his right hand clenched like the hand of the image of Gopala. She was amazed and caught hold of the hand, whereupon the figure vanished and in its place the real Gopala appeared. She cried aloud with joy. Gopala begged her for butter. She pleaded her poverty and gave Him some dry coconut candies. Gopala sat on her lap, snatched away her rosary, jumped on her shoulders and moved all about the room. As soon as day broke, she hastened to Dakshineswar like an insane woman. Of course, Gopala accompanied her, resting His head on her shoulder. She clearly saw His tiny, ruddy feet hanging over her breast. She entered Sri Ramakrishna's room. The Master had fallen into samadhi. Like a child he sat on her lap and she began to feed him butter, cream and other delicacies. After some time he regained consciousness and returned to his bed. But the mind of Gopala's mother was still roaming in another plane. After all, who saw Gopala frequently entering the Master's body and coming out of it?

When she returned to her hut, still in a dazed condition, Gopala accompanied her.

She spent about two months in uninterrupted communion with God – the Baby Gopala never leaving her for a moment. Then, the intensity of her vision lessened. If it hadn't, her body would have perished. The Master spoke highly of her exalted spiritual condition and said that such a vision of God was a rare experience for ordinary mortals.

One day, the fun-loving Master confronted the critical Narendranath with this simple-minded woman. No two individuals could have presented a more striking contrast. The Master knew of Narendra's lofty contempt for all visions, but he asked the old lady to narrate her experiences. With great hesitation she recited her story. Now and then she interrupted her maternal chatter to ask Narendra, 'My son, I am a poor ignorant woman. I don't understand anything. You are so learned. Now, tell me if these visions of Gopala are true.' As Narendra listened to the story he was profoundly moved. He said, 'Yes, mother, they are quite true.' This clearly depicted that behind his cynicism, Narendra too, possessed a heart full of love and tenderness.

Gopal Ma was with Sri Ramakrishna till the end of his days. She would assist Saradamani in her household duties. His other women disciples included Gauri Ma who fulfilled Sri Ramakrishna's vision of the upliftment of Indian women and Yogin Ma who lived in Baghbazaar in Calcutta. Sri Ramakrishna called her a *jnani*. She too was with Sri Ramakrishna during his last days in Kasipur.

Then there was Sri Ramakrishna's niece, Lakshmi Devi (1864–1926), the daughter of Rameshwar. Soon after her marriage she became a widow and went to live at Dakshineswar to assist Saradamani in the care of the Master. In the later part of her life, she drew many disciples around her and inspired them with stories and teachings of the Master.

An account of Sri Ramakrishna's disciples would not be complete without mention of two other important devotees, Mahendra Nath Gupta and Girish Chandra Ghosh. The former, who was the headmaster of Vidyasagar's High School in Calcutta, came down to posterity as M, under which humble name he wrote, in meticulous and faithful detail, of the last years of the Master's life. This was published eventually as *The Gospel of Sri Ramakrishna*. M came to Dakshineswar in 1882, grievously harmed by his family but with all the mental constructs of the Brahmo Samaj.

Ramakrishna asked him, 'So, you are married. Is your wife possessed of attributes leading to God?' Mahendra Nath replied, 'She is good, but she is ignorant.' Ramakrishna said sharply, 'And you are wise?' Mahendra Nath felt ashamed and the Master continued, 'What aspect of God appeals to you. With form or without?' Mahendra Nath replied seriously, 'Sir, I like to think of God as formless. It is meaningless to worship a clay image. One should explain to those who worship images that they are not God.' The Master reacted to this and said, 'Bah! It is the fashion with you Calcutta people to lecture and teach others. Who are you to teach others? The Lord of the Universe will look to that. You had better try to attain knowledge and devotion yourself.'

'One of the names of God,' said Girish Chandra Ghosh, 'is Saviour of the Fallen. I and no one else can bear witness that Sri Ramakrishna deserved that name. Some of those who have been with the Master may be fickle-minded, they may have a few weaknesses, their feet may have slipped a few times, but in comparison with my Himalayan faults, they are saints.'

Girish was a born rebel. He was a sceptic, a bohemian and a drunkard. He was also the greatest Bengali dramatist of his time, the father of the modern Bengali stage. Like other young men of his age, he had imbibed all the vices of the West, plunged into a life of dissipation and become convinced that religion was total fraud. Materialistic philosophy, he justified, enabled one to get some fun out of life. But a series of reversals shocked him and he became eager to solve the riddle of life. He had heard people say that to lead a spiritual life one needed the help of a guru. It was imperative that the guru be regarded as God Himself. But Girish was too well-acquainted with human nature to see perfection in any human being.

His first meeting with Sri Ramakrishna did not impress him at all. He returned home feeling as if he had seen a freak at a circus; for the Master, in a semi-conscious mood, had enquired whether it was evening, though the lamps were burning in the room. But their paths continued to cross and Girish could not avoid further encounters. The Master attended a performance in Girish's Star Theatre. On this occasion too, Girish found nothing impressive about him. One day, however, Girish happened to see the Master dancing and singing with his devotees. He wanted to join them, but restrained himself for fear of ridicule. Another day, as Sri Ramakrishna was about to give him spiritual instruction, Girish said, 'I don't want to listen to instructions. I have myself written many instructions. They are of no use to me. Please help me in a more tangible way, if you can.' This pleased the Master and he asked Girish to cultivate faith.

As time passed, Girish began to learn that the guru is the one who silently unfolds the disciple's inner life. He became a steadfast devotee of the Master. But he frequently insulted the Master, drank in his presence and took great liberties, which often astounded the other devotees. The Master knew that at heart Girish was tender, faithful and sincere. He would not allow Girish to give up theatre. When a devotee asked him to tell Girish to give up drinking, he sternly replied, 'That is none of your business. He who has taken charge of him will look after him. Girish is a devotee of the heroic type. I tell you, drinking will not affect him.' The Master knew that mere words could not induce a man to break deep-rooted habits, but that the silent influence of love worked miracles. Therefore, he never asked him to give up alcohol, with the result that Girish himself eventually broke the habit. Sri Ramakrishna strengthened Girish's resolution by allowing him to feel that he was absolutely free to do anything he wanted and did not create any bonds for him.

Atheism was the fashion of the day. Belief in the existence of God was considered a sign of weakness. After reading a few pages of science people jumped to the conclusion that religion was pure imagination and myth; priests had concocted it to frighten people into morality and abstention. Wisdom lay in accomplishing one's ends by any means. An unworthy act became ignoble only when it was discovered. It was daylight that made sin, to fulfil one's purpose secretly was proof of talent and to satisfy one's desire through cleverness was a mark of intelligence.

In a world ruled by providence, such intelligence does not last. When evil deeds bear fruit, hard lessons are learned – the hard way. Even by talented, intelligent actors and playwrights such as Girish Chandra Ghosh.

One day, when Ramakrishna was sitting with Niranjan and Ramlal, Girish entered in a drunken state, staggered, went up to the Master and said, 'You are the Saviour of the Fallen.' He sat at his feet while the devotees around were aghast, and again told the Master, 'Why don't you ask me about my past? You ask everybody about their past.' The Master looked at him neutrally, and said, 'I don't need to ask. You are made of glass.' Girish boastfully admitted that he had drunk so much in his life that if the bottles were to be placed one upon another, they would reach as high as Mount Everest. The Master said, 'And you want to drink more?' Girish nodded his head emphatically and said, 'Yes, I want to drink more.' Ramakrishna said, 'You want to drink now?' . . . and turning to Ramlal he gestured to bring the bottle and give it to Girish. Ramlal handed it over to Girish with disgust.

Niranjan was neither able to control his anger nor bear Girish's audacity to dare to drink in front of the Master. The enraged Niranjan said, 'Have you no shame, drinking at the feet of such a holy man?' Girish went out feeling ashamed, he broke the bottle and came back saying, 'I did not come here to drink. I did not.' The Master said, 'Then why did you come?' Girish pleaded, 'You are the Saviour of the Fallen. Tell me what to do.' And the Master said, 'Look at me.' Girish looked at him, barely able to focus, as he was drunk. Then he sobered down and said, 'You have spoiled the effect of a whole bottle! . . . Tell me what to do.' And the Master told him, 'Take the name of God, morning and evening.' Girish gave it a serious thought and said, 'I am not sure I can do it. I don't know in what condition or where I may be at those hours. I don't want to promise anything I can't do.' The Master made a further concession and said, 'Then, remember God before you sit down for a meal and before going to bed.' 'That also I can't promise you. I have my theatre to run and I am often engrossed in lawsuits. I can't even do that,' said Girish. 'Then give me your power of attorney,' said the Master and Girish very gladly accepted the offer.

Girish Ghosh had not realized that giving a power of attorney as an act of love would be a hundred times more binding than succumbing to a set of rules. He went about his business without anxiety, sure that Sri Ramakrishna had taken over responsibility for his spiritual life. But he was not to know on what paths his mentor would lead him, which he would necessarily have to follow.

Over time he realized that established spiritual practices such as *japa* have an end, but there is no end to the work of one who has given a power of attorney, for he must watch every step and every breath, for they now, at all times, depended on, and were available to, the Supreme. The unlikely Ghosh was to become one of Sri Ramakrishna's more famous followers, loyal, faithful, devoted, even after the Master attained *mahasamadhi*.

And so they came over the next six years, disciples and devotees, until their numbers all but eclipsed the physical presence of the Master. They came from all levels of society, at all ages, from all professions, at different stages of evolution, with their individual stories and dreams. In each, Sri Ramakrishna discerned that spark of yearning for the Divine, sometimes hidden, sometimes evident, that would mark them off from the ordinary man, to form what would become the Ramakrishna Order after the passing away of the Master.

And all the while, Sri Ramakrishna shared himself generously, speaking endlessly of the realizations on the nature of the universe, given to him in sadhana and samadhi, dancing in ecstasy, giving freely of himself to even more devotees. The Master said to all of them:

> Strike a balance between free will and predestination, self-effort and surrender. Just as when a cow is tied to a post with a long tether, she can stand one cubit from the post or she can choose to go as far as the tether allows. Such is the free will of man.

Eight

Mahasamadhi

I tried to find the Eternal in my thoughts
But it is beyond the mind to comprehend.
My mind sees this plainly
But alas, my heart will not be satisfied.

Cossipore Garden House

One day in January 1884, the Master was going towards the pine grove when he suddenly went into samadhi. As he walked all by himself there was no one around to support him or guide his footsteps. He fell to the ground and dislocated a bone in his left arm. This accident had a significant influence on his mind. Consequently, his natural inclination soared above the consciousness of the body. The acute pain in the arm forced his mind to dwell on the body and on the world outside. But he saw a Divine purpose even in this accident. As his mind compelled him to dwell on the physical plane, he realized that he was an instrument in the hand of the Divine Mother, who had to fulfil a mission through his human body and mind.

He also distinctly found that God manifested Himself in an inscrutable way through diverse human beings – both good and evil. Thus he spoke of God in the guise of the wicked, the pious, the hypocrite and the lewd. He began to take a special delight in watching the Divine Play in the relative world. Sometimes the sweet, human relationship with God appeared more appealing than the all-effecting knowledge of Brahman. He often prayed:

Mother, don't make me unconscious through the knowledge of Brahman. Don't give me *Brahmajnana*, Mother. Am I not your child, and naturally timid? I must have my Mother. A million salutations to the knowledge of Brahman! Give it to those who want it.

Sri Ramakrishna dancing in divine ecstasy   (*Sketch by* Nandlal Bose)

Again he prayed, 'O Mother! Let me remain in contact with men. Don't make me a dried-up ascetic. I want to enjoy your sport in the world.' He tasted this rich and Divine experience as well as he enjoyed the love of God and the company of His devotees, because his mind was forced to come down to the consciousness of the body on account of the injury to his arm. Again he made fun of people who proclaimed him a Divine incarnation by pointing to his broken arm, saying, 'Have you ever heard of God breaking His arm?' It took the arm about five months to heal.

In April 1885, the Master suffered from another physical ailment. His throat became inflamed. Prolonged conversation or absorption in samadhi would aggravate the pain making the blood flow into the throat. Yet when the annual Vaishnava festival was celebrated at Panihati, near Calcutta, Sri Ramakrishna attended it against the doctor's advice. With a group of disciples he spent himself in music, dance and ecstasy.

During the festival, the Vaishnavas sang and Sri Ramakrishna listened to them with rapt attention almost on the brink of another spiritual rapture. Sitting along with him were Sarat, Yogin, Yogin Ma and Naren. Among the devotees was a man dressed in Vaishnavite garb who caught Naren's eye. Naren thought he was a fake and a hypocrite. He tried to stop the devotees' playacting but could not as Ramakrishna went into samadhi and began to dance with extraordinary power and beauty. One could see the radiance that seemed to grow all around him. The singers were singing:

O Nitai giver of love is come!
Here's Nitai bringing love Divine.
Our longing hearts could not be appeased without him.
Here's Nitai our giver of love.

When Ramakrishna joined the song the hypocrite put food in his mouth. The Master instantly shuddered and spat the food out. Naren, who was watching all this, tried to pull the Master away but could not. The devotees fell at his feet and touched him. It is said that the man who gained enlightenment by Sri Ramakrishna's touch that day spent the rest of his life in contemplation of the Almighty.

The illness took a turn for the worse and was diagnosed as 'clergyman's sore throat'. The patient was cautioned against conversation and ecstasies. Though he followed the physician's directions regarding medicine and diet, he was neither able to control his samadhi nor withhold the solace of his advice to the seekers. Sometimes, like a sullen child, he complained to the Mother about the crowds who gave him no rest – day or night. His devotees overheard him saying to Goddess Kali, 'Why do You bring all these worthless people here who are like milk diluted with five times its own quantity of water? My eyes are almost destroyed with blowing the fire to dry up the water. My health is gone. It is beyond my strength. Do it Yourself, if You want it done. This (pointing to his own body) is but a perforated drum, and if You keep beating it day in and day out, how long will it last?'

But this large heart never turned anyone away. He said, 'Let me be condemned to be born over and over again even in the form of a dog, if I can be of help to a single soul.' And he bore the pain and sang cheerfully, 'Let the body be preoccupied with illness, but, O mind, dwell forever in God's Bliss!'

Towards the beginning of September 1885, Sri Ramakrishna suffered a haemorrhage of the throat. The doctor now diagnosed the illness as cancer. Narendra broke this heart-rending news to the disciples. Within three days the Master was moved to Calcutta for better treatment. He remained at Balaram's house for a week till a suitable place was found at Shyampukur, in North Calcutta. The whole of the following week he dedicated himself – practically without respite – to the instruction of those devotees who had been unable to visit him often at Dakshineswar. Discourses incessantly flowed from his tongue, and he often went into samadhi. Dr Mahendra Sarkar, the celebrated homeopath doctor who founded the Society for Science where C.V. Raman worked, was also invited to undertake his treatment.

Narendra organized the young disciples to attend to the Master day and night. At first they concealed the Master's illness from their guardians, but when it became more serious they remained with him almost constantly, sweeping aside the objections of their relatives and devoting themselves whole-heartedly to the nursing of their beloved guru. These young men, under the watchful eyes of the Master and the leadership of Narendra, became the *antaranga bhaktas*, the devotees of Sri Ramakrishna's inner circle. They were the privileged ones and witnessed many manifestations of the Master's Divine powers. It was Narendra who received instructions regarding the propagation of his message after his death.

The Holy Mother – as Sarada Devi had come to be affectionately known by Sri Ramakrishna's devotees – was brought from Dakshineswar to look after him – to prepare the special diet of the patient. Since the dwelling space was extremely limited, she had to adapt herself to cramped conditions. At three o'clock in the morning she finished her bath in the Ganga and then entered a small covered place on the terrace of the house, where she spent the whole day cooking and praying. Only once all the visitors left for the night – which never happened before eleven at night – she came down to her small bedroom to rest for a few hours. Thus, she spent three months and worked hard, slept little and prayed constantly for the Master's recovery.

At Shyampukur, the devotees led an intense life. The way they attended to their Master was in itself a form of spiritual discipline. During this period, Sri Ramakrishna's mind was soaring on an exalted plane of consciousness. Occasionally they caught a glimpse of his spiritual fervour. They sought to find the meaning of their Master's illness, which was making him physically weak, since most of them accepted him as an incarnation of God. One group headed by Girish, with his robust optimism and great power of imagination, believed that the illness was a mere pretext to serve a deeper purpose. The Master had willed his illness in order to bring the devotees together and promote solidarity among them. As soon as this purpose was served he would himself get rid of the disease. A second group thought that the Divine Mother, in whose hands the Master was an instrument, had brought about this illness to serve Her own mysterious ends. But the young rationalists led by Narendra refused to ascribe a supernatural cause to a natural phenomenon. They believed that it was to him alone they must look for the attainment of their spiritual goal.

In spite of the physician's best efforts, the prayers and nursing of the devotees, the illness progressed rapidly. Sometimes the pain appeared to be unbearable. The Master lived on liquid food and his frail body was becoming a mere shadow of his former self. Yet his face always radiated joy and he continued to welcome the visitors pouring in to receive his blessing. When certain zealous devotees tried to keep the visitors away, they were told by Girish, 'You cannot succeed in this, he has been born for this very purpose to sacrifice himself for the redemption of others.'

As time passed, the Master's health deteriorated further. Once when he was lying on his bed with a poultice around his throat surrounded by Naren, the doctor and other devotees, Sarada brought in milk and *dalia* to feed him. Just then Naren told him, 'The veranda is full of devotees. There are crowds three deep beyond.' Ramakrishna said enthusiastically, 'Give me a moment. I will speak to them.' The doctor tried to stop him from going. Sri Ramakrishna looked at him as though he was mad. He got up and tottered out.

The more the disease strengthened its hold, the more the body was devastated by illness, the more it became the habitation of the Divine spirit. Through its transparency, the gods and goddesses shone with ever-increasing luminosity. On the day of the Kali Puja, the devotees vividly saw in him the manifestation of the Divine Mother.

Around this time it was noticed that some of the devotees were making an unbridled display of their emotions. A number of them, particularly the householders, began to cultivate – at first unconsciously – the art of shedding tears. They even shook their bodies, contorted their faces, and went into trances, thereby attempting to imitate the Master. They began to openly declare Sri Ramakrishna a Divine incarnation and to regard themselves as his chosen people, who could neglect religious disciplines with impunity. Narendra's sharp eyes soon sized up the situation. He found out that some of these external manifestations were being carefully practised at home, while some were the outcome of malnutrition, mental weakness or nervous debility. Mercilessly, he exposed those who pretended to have visions and asked all of them to develop a healthy, religious spirit. Narendra sang inspiring songs for the younger devotees, read with them the words of Christ and the Gita, and held before them the positive ideals of spirituality.

One day in the Shyampukur street house, Naren and Girish Ghosh were talking outside the Master's room and Girish Ghosh very dramatically said, 'Believe me, the Master is a Divine incarnation, so he's not subject to karma. If he's sick it's for some purpose of his own; it's playacting. As soon as his purpose has been fulfilled, he'll get well.'

Gopalchandra Ghosh disagreed. 'Everything to you is theatre, Babu. No, no. The Master has always said he's the child and instrument of the Divine Mother. So it is She who has made him sick, for Her own purpose. Perhaps for the good of humanity. When Her purpose has been served, he'll get well.'

And Naren said, 'Look, I have no doubt the Master's is a Divine spirit. But surely you can see the distinction between a divine spirit and a mortal body! Mortal bodies can be healed by human science.'

One day after seeing the patient, Dr Sarkar came out of Ramakrishna's room, shook his head in disappointment and told Naren who was waiting outside, 'I cannot stop him from talking. You must keep all these people away from him. He's in Calcutta for a cure, not to be more easily accessible!' He paused and looked at Naren. 'I believe the expenses of the Master's illness are being borne by the devotees?'

Naren nodded. Dr Sarkar said, 'And I'm told some of you are mortgaging your houses, selling ornaments and rationing food for your children?' Again Naren nodded. Dr Sarkar continued, 'Then I will not take any fees from you for my services. No, no. It's not because I think he's Divine, don't mistake me . . . but . . . I must tell you, what he has to say has captured my heart.'

Naren asked abruptly, 'Is it curable?' The doctor answered, 'At first I was hopeful. But now I am not.' Meanwhile, the Master lay in bed and the devotees kept streaming in to seek his blessings.

Those who have purity from sadhanas and samadhis have body systems so finely tuned they gain *siddhis*, like the ability to heal by touch. Sri Ramakrishna reported one day that he had seen his subtle body in front of him. All along the back of this body there were deep, dark sores. When questioned, the Divine Mother explained that when people who had done many evil deeds touched him, they gained good karma from him and passed their own impurities into his body. To this the Master responded, 'Would that I could be born a thousand times so I could help humanity in this way!'

Naren was very concerned and said, 'In that case we cannot allow people to touch you, Master.' But Girish chided Naren, 'How can you stop him? That's what he was born for.'

Despite Naren's best efforts the Master was not able to get the required rest and the devotees continued to pour in. One day a devotee was singing a song from a composition by Ramprasad:

I tried to find the Eternal in my thoughts
But it is beyond the mind to comprehend.
My mind sees this plainly
But alas, my heart will not be satisfied.

Hearing these words, Ramakrishna went into samadhi. Dr Sarkar who was attending on him, bent and examined him and said, 'Clinically he's dead. There is no breath, no heartbeat, no vital signs whatever.' Naren answered, 'No Doctor, he's in samadhi. His mind is one with the Absolute. He will return to his body in time.' The doctor who was unused to such happenings, said medical science had no understanding or explanation of this phenomenon and at that same moment Sri Ramakrishna opened his eyes and smiled, much to the bewilderment of the doctor.

One day a young man in European clothes slipped inside the door as a young devotee in robes. The devotee who was actually a woman dressed in man's attire, ran up to Sri Ramakrishna and said, 'Master, do you remember me? Binodini? I acted in Babu's "Chaitanya Lila". You came backstage to congratulate me.' Ramakrishna, who remembered the woman as Binodini, smiled. She continued, 'I knew they would not allow an actress to come to you – we're considered . . . well . . . so I . . . Master . . . I needed to see you. When I touched your feet at the theatre, I . . . understood so much. I needed . . . Master you're sick. I had to . . .'

The Master laughed and said, 'If I were setting the rules here, the actress of "Chaitanya Lila" would get priority over the [speaking in English] all-important English . . . Come tell me what you want . . . You are a rascal. What a good trick. Naren will enjoy the story.'

Binodini came up and sat by Sri Ramakrishna's bed and pleaded, 'I want to realize God. I have committed great sins.' The Master assured her that the Mother forgave her erring daughters if they repented sincerely and longed for her love. 'Sincerity and practice . . . nothing more is needed.' Binodini asked earnestly what scriptures she should read, so the Master lovingly told her, 'When you know the Absolute, scriptures are worth nothing. A tiny ray of light from the Divine Mother makes all learning pale into insignificance. Attachment to lust and wealth binds the soul.'

Binodini touched her head to his feet and took leave of him in a state of bliss.

On another occasion, Pandit Shashadhar, Dr Sarkar, Naren and Latu were standing by the bedside of the Master, and Pandit Shashadhar told the Master, 'The scriptures tell us that a Paramahamsa like yourself can cure himself by his own will power by concentrating his mind at the point of the illness. Why don't you do this?' Sri Ramakrishna was surprised at this and said, 'Shashadhar, you call yourself a pandit, yet you can make such a suggestion? This mind has been given to God. How can I recall it and make it dwell in this dilapidated cage of flesh and bones?' But Naren pleaded, 'For our sake if not your own. Will you do it?' Latu joined in, 'Please, Master!' Dr Sarkar added, 'Yes. For us if not for you.' Then Sri Ramakrishna told them, 'Do you think I'm suffering like this because I want to?' Dr Sarkar anxiously asked, 'Master, did you pray to the Divine Mother?'

Ramakrishna nodded his head and said, 'Yes I did and I told the Divine Mother that I can't eat anything because of this pain, Mother. Please let me eat a little. But she pointed to all of you and said, "Why, you're eating through so many mouths already." Then I was so ashamed I could not utter another word.'

And the disciples too, hung their heads in shame.

The Master's condition deteriorated further, and Dr Sarkar suggested a move out of polluted Calcutta. The house at Kashipur Gardens was dilapidated and expensive. Sri Ramakrishna asked Surendra Nath Mitra, one of his earliest followers, who had been cured of his destructive desire for alcohol and women, to take over the entire financial burden to ease the less affluent devotees; Mitra complied gladly. The Master was moved to Kashipur on 11 December 1885.

It was here that the curtain fell on the varied activities of the Master's life, on the physical plane. His soul lingered in the mortal body for eight more months. It was a period of great passion for him. On the one hand, there was a constant crucifixion of the body and on the other, there was the triumphant revelation of the soul. Here the devotees witnessed first-hand the humanity and divinity of the Master cross a thin borderline again and again. Every minute of those eight months was suffused with touching tenderness of the heart and breathtaking elevation of spirit. Every word he uttered was full of pathos and sublimity.

It took the group only a few days to get adjusted to the new environment. The Holy Mother, assisted by Sri Ramakrishna's niece, Lakshmi Devi, and a few other women devotees, took charge of the cooking for the Master and his attendants. Surendra willingly bore the major portion of the expenses while other householders contributed according to their means. The twelve disciples who were constant attendants of the Master were: Narendra, Rakhal, Baburam, Niranjan, Jogin, Latu, Tarak, the elder Gopal, Kali, Sashi, Sarat and the younger Gopal. Sarada, Harish, Hari, Gangadhar and Tulasi visited the Master often and practised sadhana at home. Narendra, preparing for his law examination, brought his books to the garden house in order to continue his studies during the infrequent spare moments. He encouraged the other disciples to intensify their meditation, scriptural studies and other spiritual disciplines. Immersed in their devotion they forgot the outside world and their worldly duties.

Among the attendants, Sashi was the embodiment of service. He did not practise meditation, *japa* or any of the other disciplines followed by the other devotees. He was convinced that service to the guru was the only religion for him. He sometimes even forgot to eat or rest and was ever ready at the Master's bedside.

The move to Kashipur Gardens had the effect of consolidating the group that would in the months to come form the Ramakrishna Order. As the house was so far out of Calcutta, the disciples had to move and live there in order to look after the Master. The Master had said in one of his discourses at Dakshineswar, 'This body will cease to exist by the Mother's will. At that time it will be shown which devotees belong to the inner circle and which to the outer.' Now at Kashipur he clarified, 'When many people start to whisper about *how I am*,' he said, 'the devotees are being sifted by this illness. Those who are living here, renouncing the world, belong to the inner circle; and those who pay occasional visits and ask "How are you, Sir?" – they belong to the outer.'

One day, as Naren strolled in the garden he ran into other disciples and they began to talk to each other. Naren told them:

The Master may have decided to abandon his body. So, let us make as much spiritual progress as we can with meditation and service. Otherwise, when he leaves us, how shall we ever forgive ourselves? Are we going to put off calling the name of the Lord until our worldly desires are satisfied? See how we're letting the days slip by. We're getting more and more tied up in this net of desires. Let us give them up! Yes, let us give them all up!

Naren picked up some dried leaves and branches from under the tree and said, 'Let us set fire to them. Holy men light *dhuni* fires at this time of night to burn up their desires. Let's do the same.'

Before the Master became ill he had said, 'I shall make the whole thing public before I go.' On 1 January 1886, Sri Ramakrishna felt better and went down to the garden for a brief stroll. It was about three o'clock in the afternoon. About thirty lay disciples were present in the hall, while some sat under the trees. Sri Ramakrishna told Girish, 'Well, Girish, what have you seen in me, that you proclaim me, before everybody, as an incarnation of God?' Girish was not a man who was often taken by surprise. He apologized with folded hands to the Master for the liberties that he had taken. The Master forgave him and said, 'I bless you all. Be illumined!' And he fell into a spiritual mood. When the devotees heard these words, one and all were overwhelmed with emotion. They rushed to him and fell at his feet. He touched them all and each received an appropriate benediction. Every one of them, at the touch of the Master, experienced ineffable bliss – while some laughed, some wept, some sat down to meditate and others began to pray. Some of them saw light, some had visions of their chosen ideals, and some felt within their bodies the rush of spiritual power.

The Master did not hide the fact that he wished to make Narendra his spiritual heir and Narendra continued the work after Sri Ramakrishna's passing. Sri Ramakrishna told him, 'I leave these young men in your charge. See that they develop their spirituality and do not return home.' One day he asked the boys, in preparation for a monastic life, to beg for their food from door to door without any regard to caste. They hailed the Master's order and went out with begging bowls. A few days later he gave the cloth of the sannyasi to each of those disciples, including Girish, who was now second to none in his spirit of renunciation. Thus, the Master himself laid the foundation of the future Ramakrishna Order of monks.

Sri Ramakrishna was sinking day by day. His diet was reduced to a minimum and he found it almost impossible to swallow. He whispered to Mother, 'I am bearing all this cheerfully, for otherwise you would be weeping. If you all say that it is better that the body should go rather than suffer this torture, I am willing.' The next morning he told his depressed disciples seated near the bed, 'Do you know what I see? I see that God alone has become everything. Men and animals are only frameworks covered with skin, and it is He who is moving through their heads and limbs. I see that it is God Himself who has become the block, the executioner and the victim for the sacrifice.'

He fainted with emotion. Regaining partial consciousness, he said, 'Now I have no pain. I am very well.' Looking at Latu, he said, 'There sits Latu resting his head on the palm of his hand. To me it is the Lord who is seated in that posture.'

The words were tender and touching. Like a mother he caressed Narendra and Rakhal, gently stroking their faces. He spoke in a half whisper to Mother, 'Had this body been allowed to last a little longer, many more souls would have been illuminated.' He paused a moment and then said, 'But Mother has ordained otherwise. Take me away, lest finding me guileless and foolish, people should take advantage of me and persuade me to bestow on them the rare gift of spirituality.'

A few minutes later he touched his chest and said, 'Here fare two beings. One is She and the other is Her devotee. It is he who broke his arm, and it is he again who is now ill. Do you understand me?' After a pause he added 'Alas! To whom shall I tell all this? Who will understand me?'

'Pain,' he consoled them again, 'is unavoidable as long as there is a body. The Lord takes on the body for the sake of His devotees.'

Yet one is not sure whether the Master's soul was actually tortured by this agonizing disease. At least during his moments of spiritual exaltation – that became constant during the last days of his life on earth – he lost all consciousness of the body, illness and suffering. One of his attendants said later, 'While Sri Ramakrishna lay sick he never actually suffered pain. He would often say: "O mind! Forget the body, forget the sickness, and remain merged in Bliss." No, he did not really suffer. At times he would be in a state when the thrill of joy was clearly manifested in his body. Even when he could not speak, he would let us know in some way that there was no suffering and this fact was clearly evident to all who watched him. People who did not understand him thought that his suffering was very great. Spiritual joy was clearly manifested in his body. What spiritual joy he transmitted to us at that time! Could such a thing have been possible if he had been suffering physically? It was during this period that he taught us again these truths: "Brahman is always unattached. The three *gunas* are in it, but it is unaffected by them, just as the wind carries odour, yet remains odourless. Brahman is infinite being, infinite wisdom, infinite bliss. In it there exists no delusion, no misery, no disease, no death, no growth and no decay. The transcendental being and the being within are one and the same. There is one indivisible, absolute existence."'

Sarada Ma secretly went to the Shiva temple across the Ganga to intercede with the Deity for the Master's recovery. In a revelation she was told to prepare herself for the inevitable end.

One day, while Naren was sitting by the bed of the Master and as a burning desire for realization overwhelmed him, he said to the Master, 'Please permit me a realization. Everyone else has had theirs. Why not me? I sit with you every night for three hours, while you teach me. Yet I have not had a sight of the Supreme.' The Master told him, 'You should settle your family affairs. Then you will have everything. But what is it you want?' Naren said, 'I want to be in samadhi for a long time.' The Master reprimanded him, 'You are a fool. There's a higher plane than that. You keep singing: "All that exists art Thou." A samadhi is temporary and from it one must come down. Ordinary men may reach samadhi. But only an Ishwarkoti can continually see that God exists in the manifested universe.'

Just then Mother Sarada entered to clean up after giving the Master some gruel and the Master told her, 'They don't tell me how long it will take me to recover. How is it that I have all these ecstasies and visions and samadhis, and yet I'm so ill? It was revealed to me in a vision that during my last days I would have to live on pudding.'

And he continued with tears in his eyes, 'Is this what it meant? And so painfully too?'

Mother Sarada stopped cleaning and looked at him and he continued, 'Look here. You will have to learn to do something too, this body cannot do everything.' Mother Sarada got frightened and said, 'No. No. I'm only a woman. I cannot do anything.' The Master replied, 'No. That will not do. You will have to learn to do many things. It is the will of the Divine Mother that when I am gone you have much to do.' And he gave her instructions.

Once while Naren was meditating, he suddenly shouted, 'Where is my body? I can't feel my body.' When Gopal heard him shout, he ran in and said, 'Here, Naren.' Naren continued, 'I can't feel my body. I only have a head.' And Gopal helplessly ran to the Master and reported, 'Naren cannot feel his body. He is losing consciousness.' So the Master answered, 'He is in *nirvikalpa*. Let him be for a while. He has teased me long enough for it!' Naren settled down after a while and went to the Master's room and the Master said, 'Now Mother has shown you everything. But this will be kept shut up in a box like a jewel and I will keep the key. When your work on earth is done, the box will be unlocked and you will know everything you knew, just now. You will know who you are and will voluntarily give up your body. But now your work is to shake the world with your intellect and spiritual power.'

Naren, who was a sceptic, was still doubtful about his Master and as he massaged the Master's feet he said to himself, 'If in the midst of this dreadful physical pain, he can declare his Godhead, then I shall believe him.' And the Master whose eyes were closed and who was also in great pain indicated to his body with tremendous effort and said in a clear voice, 'Why Naren! Do you still doubt me? The one who became Rama and he who was Krishna is now within this sheath . . . But not according to your Vedanta!' Naren was moved by this final affirmation. He broke down and wept grievously.

When the Master was sinking, Mother Sarada wept by his bedside. The Master told her, 'You mustn't be anxious. Your life will be just the same. Naren and the others will look after you. They'll be as good to you as you have been to me.'

Some days later, while Narendra was alone with the Master, Sri Ramakrishna looked at him and went into samadhi. Narendra felt the penetration of a subtle force and lost all outer consciousness. When he regained consciousness, he found the Master weeping.

Sri Ramakrishna said to him, 'Today I have given you my all and I am now only a poor fakir, possessing nothing. By this power you will do immense good in the world, and not till it is accomplished will you return.' Henceforth, the Master lived in the disciple.

On Sunday, 15 August 1886 the Master's pulse became irregular. The devotees stood by the bedside. Towards dusk, Sri Ramakrishna had difficulty in breathing. A short time later he complained of hunger. A little liquid food was put into his mouth; some of it he swallowed, while the rest ran down his chin. Two attendants began to make fun of him. All at once he went into samadhi of a rather unusual type. The body became stiff. Sashi burst into tears. But after midnight the Master revived.

He was now very hungry and helped himself to a bowl of porridge and said he was strong again. He sat up and several pillows were propped behind him for support. Sashi was next to him, fanning him. Narendra placed the Master's feet on his lap and rubbed them. Repeatedly the Master told him, 'Take care of these boys.' Then he lay down. He cried the name of Kali, his life's Beloved, three times in ringing tones, and lay back.

At two minutes past one, early on Monday morning, 16 August 1886, something passed over his body. His hair stood on end. His eyes were fixed on the tip of his nose. His face was illuminated with a smile. The final ecstasy had begun. It was the *mahasamadhi*, total absorption, from which his mind never returned. Narendra, unable to bear it, ran downstairs. But the devotees were unwilling to admit that the Master was no more. Through the night they watched and waited for the Master to return. Dr Sarkar arrived the following noon and pronounced that life had departed not more than half an hour before.

At five o'clock, the Master's body was taken downstairs, laid on a cot, dressed in ochre clothes, and decorated with sandal paste and flowers. A procession was taken out. Passers-by wept as the body was taken to the cremation ground at the ghat on the Ganga and cremated there, almost directly across the river from the spot on which stands the great Belur Math today.

When the devotees returned to the garden house and carried the urn with the sacred ashes, a calm resignation came to their souls and they cried, 'Victory unto the Guru!'

The Holy Mother wept in her room, not for her husband but because she felt that Mother Kali had left her. When she was about to wear a pristine white sari and don the marks of a Hindu widow, in a moment of revelation she heard the words of faith, 'I have only passed from one room to another.'

Glossary

Achaitanya	:	Unconscious
Adharma	:	Opposite of dharma, see Dharma
Adhyatma Ramayana	:	The Ramayana is a mythological story of the Hindu tradition which chronicles the story of Lord Rama. The Adhyatma Ramayana is a text which deals with the philosophy of the story.
Advaita	:	A religious philosophy which expounds absolute Non-dualism
Advaitin	:	One who sees no difference between God and his creation
Allah	:	Supreme Godhead according to the tradition of Islam
Amalaki	:	Indian gooseberry
Anahata dhvani	:	Inner Divine Sound
Ananda	:	Bliss
Antaranga bhaktas	:	Devotees of the inner circle
Anubhava	:	Experience
Anur	:	Name of a village
Asoka	:	Name of a king who renounced conquest and took to Buddhism
Atman	:	The individual soul or jiva
Avatar	:	Hinduism believes that the Supreme God incarnates amongst men on earth and then he or she is called an avatar

Avidyamaya	: Represents the dark forces of creation
Ayurveda	: An Indian form of herbal medicine
Baba	: Father
Babu	: Equivalent to Sir
Bangla	: Language spoken by the people of eastern and western Bengal which are two states in India. East Bengal has now become an independent country (Bangladesh).
Bauls	: Baul is a form of folk music and the people who sing it are called Bauls
Belur Math	: An institution set up by Vivekananda after the passing away of Sri Ramakrishna which is close to Dakshineswar
Benares	: Originally called Kasi or Varanasi which is an important place of pilgrimage for the Hindus
Benaresi sari	: Benares has been known for producing hand woven saris for women all over India
Bengali	: The language spoken by the people of Bengal
Bhagavad Gita	: Teaching given by Lord Krishna to his disciple Arjuna on the battlefield compiled into a text
Bhairava	: A form of Shiva who represents death hence known as god of death
Bhairavi	: A female worshipper of the God of Death
Bhajan	: A form of devotional music
Bhakta	: Worshipper
Bhakti	: Intense love of God, attachment to Him alone
Bhavamukha	: On the threshold of relative consciousness
Bhavas	: Attitudes towards God
Bhavatarini	: Goddess whose grace helps us cross the ocean of mundane existence
Bhikshu/ bhiksha	: Mendicant seeking alms, ritual begging for grace of God through food
Bhoga	: Enjoyment, material life
Bhutirkhal	: Name of a cremation ground
Bodhi tree	: A peepal tree under which the Buddha attained enlightenment
Brahma	: One of the gods of the trinity who creates the manifested universe in Hindu mythology

Brahmo Samaj	: Eclectic movement in Bengal in the 19th century for the reformation of Hinduism while retaining the best of the Upanishads and combining with Christian practices
Brahmo	: A member of the Brahmo Samaj
Brahmachari	: One who seeks the Brahman by control of the senses including celibacy
Brahmajnana	: Knowledge of the higher self
Brahman	: The ultimate one with a name and form unlike ataman which is the ultimate one without name and form
Brahmani	: A female follower of the path to the experience of Brahman
Brahmin	: Priestly caste of the Hindu religion
Brahminical thread	: A cotton thread worn by the men who are formally initiated to follow the path prescribed in order to be called a Brahmin
Chaitanya	: Ecstatic singing saint of medieval times from Bengal
Chaitanya Bhagavata	: A text authored by Brindavandas Thakur on Chaitanya
Chaitanya Charitamrita	: Biography of Chaitanya
Chaitanya Lila	: Divine Sport by Chaitanya
Chamara	: A hand fan
Chit	: Consciousness
Choli	: An upper garment worn by women
Da	: Short form of elder brother
Dada	: Term used for elder brother
Dakshineswar	: A small place outside Calcutta (Kolkata) on the banks of the river Ganga where Sri Ramakrishna spent most of his living years
Dalia	: Broken wheat
Daridranarayana	: God in the form of a beggar
Dasa	: Servant
Dasa bhava	: The feeling of servitude
Dasaratha	: The king of Ayodhya and the father of Lord Rama who is considered an avatar of Vishnu
Dasya	: Servitude
Dasya bhava	: The mood of the child to his parent, or a servant to his master

Deogarh	:	Place near Bengal
Dere	:	The ancestral village of Sri Ramakrishna's father
Devi	:	Goddess
Dhani	:	Name of the lady who looked after Ramakrishna in his chilhood
Dharma	:	Virtue/god-given law of an individual's nature
Dharmapatra	:	The leaf of impartiality, used in the villages to clarify mixed opinions
Dhuni	:	Sacred fire
Dukkha	:	Pain and suffering
Dupatta/duppata	:	Veil or cloth used to cover the upper body
Durga	:	Goddess of Power, an aspect of Kali
Durga Puja	:	Ten-day festival celebrated in honour of Goddess Durga
Durva grass	:	Sacred weed or grass used during rituals
Dvaita	:	Dualism
Dvaitin	:	A Dualist
Fakir	:	A mendicant
Gadadhar	:	Another name for Lord Vishnu
Ganga Mai	:	The River Ganga who is addressed as a mother
Ganga	:	Sacred river of the Hindus
Gaya	:	A sacred place now in Bihar state
gharara/ghagra	:	Apparel worn by women
Gopis	:	Cowherd boys and girls who were playmates of Lord Krishna
Gunas	:	Attributes
Guru	:	Preceptor/ teacher/ master
Guru Ma	:	Consort or wife of the guru
Hanuman	:	Monkey-faced god who stands for chivalry and selfless service in the Hindu religion
Hara	:	A name of Shiva
Hari bol	:	A religious expression
Hari Om	:	A religious expression used to greet each other
Hooghly	:	A tributary of the Ganga that flows through Calcutta
Hookah	:	Traditional Indian smoking pipe
Howrah station	:	A railway station in Calcutta
Ishwar	:	God
Ishwarkotis	:	Category of the lord
Jain	:	A follower of Mahavir/ Mahavira

Jainism	:	The religion founded by Mahavira
Jal	:	Water
Japa	:	Chanting
Jasodha	:	Name of Lord Krishna's foster mother
Jiva	:	Living being
Jivan mukta	:	One who has transcended the body
Jnana yogi	:	One who follows the path of knowledge
Jnani	:	Wise one
Kabbalists	:	Ones who sing a form of music of the Sufi tradition (see qawalis)
Kali/Ma Kali	:	The goddess Sri Ramakrishna worshipped who represents the wrathful side of female energy or Shakti
Kalki	:	An incarnation of Vishnu
Karma	:	Action
Kamarpukur	:	The village where Ramakrishna hailed from, outside Kolkata. Pukur means pond.
Kausalya	:	Mother of lord Rama
Kayastha	:	A caste in Hinduism
King Janaka	:	Name of a king who is the father of Sita, the wife of Rama
Koran	:	Holy book of Islam
Kothi	:	Large Indian home
Krishna	:	An avatar of Vishnu and a godhead for the Hindus
Kshatriya	:	A warrior class of Hindus
Kund	:	Water body
Kundalini	:	In yogic vocabulary it is the divine power in human beings ever waiting to be kindled which rests in the base of the spine and travels to the top of the head through the psychic channels when kindled
Kuthi	:	Hut, dwelling place
Lila	:	Divine Sport
Longoti	:	A small cloth used to cover the lower body of men, also called loin-cloth
Lord Krishna	:	A perfect and complete avatar of Vishnu, considering the ten major avatars
Madhur	:	Sweetness
Madhura bhava	:	Love for the Divine Beloved
Mahabhava	:	Being absorbed in Divine ecstasy

Mahakali	:	Goddess Kali in all her attributes
Mahasamadhi	:	Death of the body of saints
Mahima Stotra	:	A hymn
Mama	:	Mother's brother
Manasaputra	:	Mind-born son
Mantras	:	Religious incantations
Maya	:	The goddess of illusions
Mayatita	:	Free of maya
Muladhara	:	A psychic energy centre situated at the base of the spine
Muni	:	A sage
Naga	:	Serpent
Naga monk	:	A class of mendicants who are usually naked
Nahabat	:	One of the bathing ghats on the River Ganga near Dakhineshwar
Nara	:	Man-god
Narayana	:	One of Vishnu's names
Narayani	:	Consort of Shiva and sister of Vishnu
Narmada	:	The name of a river
Navavidhan	:	New dispensation
Neti, neti, neti	:	Not this
Nirakara Brahman	:	Formless god
Nirguna	:	Without attributes
Nirvana	:	Enlightenment or, as in the case of Ramakrishna a bhakta, a state of God realization or a union with God
Nirvikalpa Samadhi	:	Samadhi without awareness (without consciousness) and Savikalpa Samadhi is Samadhi with awareness (with consciousness)
Nitai	:	Name of a person
Nityasiddhas	:	Born with powers with no previous sadhana
Nyasa	:	Renunciation
Om	:	Considered a celestial primodial sound
Pancha bhavas	:	Five different emotions
Panchavati	:	A place in Dakshineswar where Sri Ramakrishna went to meditate
Paramahamsa	:	The royal swan, symbol of the free flight of the soul. Holy men who have attained freedom from all attachments.

Paramatman	:	Supreme self
Peepul tree	:	A kind of large tree which is considered sacred
Prana	:	Life Energy
Parabrahman	:	Unmanifested God
Prasad	:	Sacred offering or sacred gift
Puja	:	Worship
Pandit	:	Expert in a particular field of knowledge
Puranas	:	Religious mythological Hindu texts
Purushottama	:	The supreme person
Qawwalis	:	Ecstatic group of Sufi singers
Radha	:	The beloved and devotee of Krishna
Radhakanta temple	:	Temple for Radha and Krishna
Radhika	:	Another name for Radha
Raghubir	:	Lord Rama
Rama	:	King and god who is the incarnation of Vishnu
Ramachandra	:	Another name of Lord Rama
Ramlala	:	Baby Rama
Ramprasad	:	Name of Sri Ramakrishna's brother
Rani	:	In this context a name of a lady
Rishis	:	Sages
Sadhana/sadhanas	:	The paths charted by sages in their single-minded quest for God
Sadhu	:	A person in pursuit of God or its equivalent living away from society like a mendicant
Sahasrara	:	In yogic science it is one of the chakras or energy centres perceived as a thousand-petalled lotus at the top of the head
Sakhya	:	Friendship
Sakhya bhava	:	The love of the friend
Shaktas	:	The worshippers of Shakti, the feminine aspect of God
Samadhi	:	A state of super-consciousness
Samsara	:	Samsara represents avidya, or ignorance, of one's true self, that leads to ego-consciousness of the body and the phenomenal world. It leads one to the perpetual chain of karma and reincarnation, a state of illusion known as Maya.

	It is a result of the ignorance of the True Self, Brahman, and thus the soul is led to believe in the reality of temporal, phenomenal existence.
Samskaras	: Habits inherited or acquired qualities mostly in the spiritual realm
Sanatan Dharma	: The eternal way of the ancient sages
Shankar	: Name of Lord Shiva
Sanskrit shlokas	: Hymns in Sanskrit either describing or eulogizing the divine
Sannyas	: Mendicancy
Sannyasa vows	: Vows of self-discipline taken before formally entering the path of mendicancy
Sannyasi	: The man who becomes a mendicant or renunciant
Sannyasini	: A woman mendicant or renunciant
Saraswati	: Goddess of Learning
Sat	: Being
Satchitananda	: Being and bliss
Sati	: A practice where the woman offers herself to the funeral pyre along with her husband's dead body
Savikalpa samadhi	: See Nirvikalpa samadhi
Shabda	: Sound/ spoken word
Shakti	: Feminine power
Shalagram stone	: A fossil from the ocean bed considered a substitute to Narayan lying on the cosmic ocean in His cosmic form
Shanta bhava	: Feeling of inner tranquillity
Shastras	: Rules deriving from scriptures about social norms
Shiva	: One of the gods of the trinity representing destruction and degeneration
Shodasi Puja	: The adoration of the divine virgin
Siddhis	: Psychic powers
Sikhism	: One of the religions practised in India
Sita	: Consort of Lord Rama
Sri Chaitanya	: Ecstatic singing saint of medieval times from Bengal
Sri Ramachandra	: A perfect man/a perfect ruler who hails from the Suryavansha dynasty

Sri Sri Jagadiswari Mahakali	:	Goddess Kali
Sufi	:	A follower of Sufi religion which has its origins in Islam
Sushumna	:	In yogic science it's a mystic channel carrying divine energy
Tamasika	:	Inert and gross
Tantra	:	A science which uses energies to spiritual attainment
Tantric	:	Unorthodox religious practitioner, a person who follows the path of tantra
Tarpana	:	Ritualistic offering during death rites
Thread ceremony	:	See Brahmanical thread
Tirthankara	:	Holy men from the Jain tradition
Tirthankara Mahavira	:	The founder of Jainism
Trailanga Swami	:	A great saint who lived in Benares
Tripurasundari	:	Supreme Goddess who has all the three female godheads in her – Durga, Lakshmi and Saraswati
Udbodan	:	A new beginning or event
Unmada	:	Madness for God
Upanishads	:	Philosophical texts of Hinduism mostly from the advaita philosophy
Vaid/vaidya	:	A medical practitioner
Vaishnava	:	Initiated follower of Vishnu
Vaishnavism	:	Sect of people who worship Vishnu
Vaishnavite	:	The one belonging to the Vaishnava community
Vaishnavite Shakti community	:	A sub-sect of people who use the methods of Tantra along with their devotion to Vishnu
Vatsalya	:	Motherly love
Vatsalya bhava	:	The love of the parent for the child
Vedanta	:	Philosophical teaching of the Vedas
Vedantin	:	One who follows the teaching of Vedanta
Vedas	:	The four timeless scriptures of timeless knowledge
Vidyamaya	:	The higher force of creation
Vilva/bilva	:	Sacred leaf used for the worship of Shiva, which is in the shape of a trident, symbolically represents the three aspects of time and also the Three Eyes of Shiva
Vishalakshi shrine	:	Shrine dedicated to the consort of Shiva

Vishnu	:	One of the gods in the trinity considered as the keeper of the universe unlike Brahma the creator and Shiva the annihilator
Visishtadvaita	:	Qualified Non-dualism
Vrindavan	:	The place where Lord Krishna lived and grew up as a child amongst the cowherds
Yoga	:	Union with consciousness, also a form of practice for keeping the physical, mental and emotional spheres of the human body in good health
Yogi	:	The practitioner of yoga
Yogic rites	:	Rituals concerning yogic practices

Bibliography

Sri Ramakrishna and His Divine Play by Swami Saradananda, translated by Swami Chetanananda, published by Vedanta Society of St Louis, 205, S. Skinker Blvd., St. Louis, MO 63105, USA, 2003.

Ramakrishna As We Saw Him, edited, translated and with a biographical introduction by Swami Chetanananda, published by Advaita Ashrama, Mayavati, Pithoragarh, 1999.

The Gospel of Sri Ramakrishna, volumes I and II, original in Bengali by Mahendranath Gupta (M), translation by Swami Nikhilananda, published by Sri Ramakrishna Math, Mylapore, Chennai.

Ramakrishna and His Disciples by Christopher Isherwood, published by Advaita Ashrama, Mayavati, Pithoragarh.

Life of Ramakrishna, compiled from various authentic sources, with a Foreword by Mahatma Gandhi, published by Advaita Ashrama, Mayavati, Pithoragarh.

Sri Ramakrishna – A Prophet for the New Age by Richard Schiffman, published by the Ramakrishna Mission Institute of Culture, Gol Park, Kolkata.

The Life of Ramakrishna by Romain Rolland, published by Advaita Ashrama, Mayavati, Pithoragarh.

Life of Swami Vivekananda by his Eastern and Western disciples, two volumes, published by Advaita Ashrama, Mayavati, Pithoragarh.

The Complete Works of Swami Vivekananda, 9 volumes, published by Advaita Ashrama, Mayavati, Pithoragarh.

The Life of Swami Vivekananda by Romain Rolland, published by Advaita Ashrama, Mayavati, Pithoragarh.

Living at the Source – Yoga Teachings of Vivekananda, edited by Ann Myren and Dorothy Madison, published by Advaita Ashrama, Mayavati, Pithoragarh.

Index

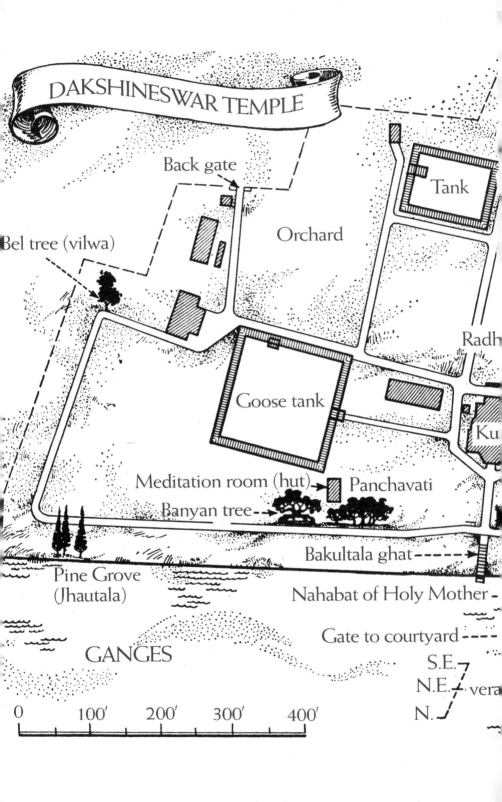

DAKSHINESWAR TEMPLE

Back gate

Orchard

Tank

Bel tree (vilwa)

Radh

Goose tank

Ku

Meditation room (hut) → Panchavati

Banyan tree →

Bakultala ghat ----→

Pine Grove
(Jhautala)

Nahabat of Holy Mother -

Gate to courtyard ----

GANGES

S.E.
N.E. ⌐ vera
N. ⌐

0   100'   200'   300'   400'